THE NEW TRUTH ABOUT DATING

NAVIGATING THE UPS AND DOWNS FOR A HEALTHY DATING LIFE

LAURA CHARANZA

The New Truth About Dating

©2022, Laura Charanza

ISBN: 978-1-66787-536-1

ISBN eBook: 978-1-66787-537-8

For Carson, I'm Your Ride or Die

CONTENTS

INTRODUCTION

I never dreamed I would be forty-four and single again, much less with an eight-year-old son. To be thrown back in the dating pool after sixteen years with the same person seemed to be a nightmare. Granted, it's not a good sign when you walk down the aisle on your wedding day thinking, "Well, if this doesn't work, I can get a divorce." That's certainly a story for another day. And if you haven't walked down the wedding aisle yet, and you are already thinking the same thought, *don't do it.* Read this book first.

Anyway, when I reentered the world of dating in 2015 after a difficult divorce, I had no idea what I would face. It had been seventeen years since I'd gone on a date with someone, and that person was my now ex-husband. We began dating in 1999, which seems like a gazillion years ago. Now, when I look back on my post-divorce dating experiences during the last seven years, I realize how much I have learned.

At first, I thought it would be easy to find a boyfriend and eventually a husband. But wow, was I wrong about that one! Dating is important so we can learn about ourselves and find someone to do life with, but if we're not careful, the process can be a soul-sucking waste of time. That's what prompted me to write this book. I want to save you the legwork and heartbreak, no matter how old are and whether you are dating the first, second, third, or fourth time around.

Think about how dating has evolved. When I was dating in my twenties, I would run home to check the answering machine or call notes to see if a certain guy had called me back. Do you remember those days? We would excitedly press play or "1," and most times, a mechanical voice would coldly say, "Hello. You have NO new messages." On a good evening, we would receive something like, "Hello. You have seven new messages." Whenever I heard this, I crossed my fingers hoping the messages weren't all from my mother.

Times have changed when it comes to technology, and therefore dating. It seems as if there are fewer people who have met their forever love in a bar and exchanged "home" numbers. Almost everyone has cell phones, and more people than ever are meeting through online dating apps instead of bars, church, or work.

You can go to a bar and hope to meet one person in an evening. Unfortunately, that one single person may be a total dimwit or loser. (Don't get mad at me. I promised to keep it real.) But today you have the option of jumping onto any given dating app and swiping through hundreds of people in minutes and perhaps connecting with a few of them.

In a recent study done at Stanford University, researchers found that 39 percent of couples today meet online. [1] Data compiled by researchers at https://www.businessofapps.com says over three hundred million people in the world use dating apps to meet possible partners. [2] Why are the numbers so large? Besides being a quick and convenient method to meet people, another reason is that we are accessible all the time. Our phones are glued to our sides, with Americans checking their messages an average of once every four minutes. It's easy to stay in touch.

What does this dating world look like on your phone? In addition to dating apps like Bumble and Tinder, there's also Match, Plenty of Fish, Farmers Only, and more. People typically meet through text messages and FaceTime calls before ever meeting in person. Connecting through electronic means permeates our dating world now.

However, despite the modern technological progress, dating issues haven't evolved into being easier to handle. Sometimes it may even seem like technology has caused us to regress when it comes to communicating. Texting has taken the place of phone calls, and ghosting is at an all- time high. Sure, typical dating issues still exist, including the possibility that a love interest might not call or text back. There's also the age-old worry that a date will be terrible or a waste of time. Finally, heartbreak or breaking someone's heart is still an everyday possibility. What makes it easier and more difficult at the same time is that breaking up or disappearing can be done by phone call or text without confronting someone in person. When someone changes their mind about a possible romantic partner, sometimes that person will just disappear. Ghosting seems to be part of the new norm, especially on dating apps.

It's important to remember this isn't all bad. Yes, the older we are the more baggage we carry, but we also are more resolute in what we want. For example, if someone ghosts me, then reappears without an explanation (this is called submarining), I don't respond. This lack of effort to be transparent doesn't work for me. I don't want someone flakey in my life. If they are inconsistent early on, what will happen a few months from now? If I am not at or near the top of their list of dating interests, then I keep it moving. We deserve more than that.

People haven't evolved in some aspects of dating because we are human, not superheroes who never age or feel. No one can take away our emotions and physical needs. Generation after generation has experienced heartbreak, pain, infidelity, marriage, divorce, and single parenting. Even my sweet grandmother shared stories of heartbreak with me before she passed away. But what has changed is the venue where someone can show character and communication skills or, as I will teach you, their lack of integrity and strength.

Dating isn't all bad! In fact, it can be exhilarating and full of positive experiences. You can go on a journey like no other and have it end in meeting the love of your life. That's what we want, right? Even after having experienced an abusive marriage, I believe in true love. You can call me an optimist if you like, but I have faith in unconditional love. I've experienced it, and there's nothing like it in the world. With this book, I'm going to help you find it.

Here's what I need you to do: read every chapter and take the steps I encourage you to take. I want you to get rid of the junk from your past, and then I'm going to teach you how to date. I'm going to teach you the secrets to attracting a healthy match and to letting the unhealthy go. I'll also instruct you on how to navigate the dating app algorithms, and I'll help you build your own process to narrow down the dating field. You'll date smart, not hard.

Count your blessings now, even before we begin. You are fortunate. Appreciate what you have because that opens the door for greater things.

Hang on tight. Follow my guidance, and you can change your life in a short amount of time. Dating will no longer be a painful process of difficulties but a slow, steady ride toward finding your soulmate.

CHAPTER 1

BEING A HEARTBREAKER, NOT HEARTBROKEN

I thought dating would be easy the second time around, but I quickly learned it can be an emotional roller coaster if not a s*#t show. Dating issues such as poor communication and heartbreak have always existed, but advancements in technology now contribute to the difficulty in finding a soulmate.

Technology makes it easy for single men and women to look at relationships and people as disposable because there's the illusion of an endless stream of choices. It seems like technology has ripped away humanity from some people when it comes to meeting others. The growing number of dating apps has contributed to "fast in fast out" relationships, and ghosting has become the new normal. It's easier to have zero confrontation, then log into the dating app to find the next shiny thing.

The growing number of dating apps has contributed to "fast in, fast out" relationships, and ghosting has become the new normal.

The good news is that we can navigate this crazy world of dating and still find our forever love. We need to heal, change our mindsets, and develop strong boundaries. This book will teach you how to do that, plus give you an algorithm to make your dating life easier and enjoyable.

My seven years of dating, including three serious relationships, have taught me the good and bad about dating. I'll share some of my dating stories with you as well as my lessons learned. You likely need to find a box of tissue because with some of my accounts, you'll laugh until you cry. With others, you may shed tears of sadness and disbelief.

This first story is below. By the way, I've changed all names and locations to protect the identity of those involved.

Dating Story #1 – "The Cheater"

Jeffrey and I met on Bumble in early April one year. I had just about given up on dating, yet again. My heart had healed from a breakup the year before, but I just couldn't find the chemistry I wanted, despite going on at least fifty first dates.

Jeffrey's profile was simple and concise. It said he split time between homes in Dallas and Austin, where he enjoyed waterskiing and listening to live music. Jeffrey's photos were good; he had taken a professional picture in a suit, then he had posted several snapshots on the beach in a swimsuit. His profile read something like, "Never married and no kids, so I have time for a relationship."

I remember saying to myself, "Damn. This guy has a great body, but he seems a little cheesy and self-involved."

Then, I silenced my annoying, always critical voice and told it to stop being so mean. So, I swiped right on Jeffrey.

From there our relationship was a whirlwind (Red Flag #1: When people move too quickly, they are often trying to hide something. They want to win you over before you figure it out). Jeffrey called, and we met for a drink the next evening. Jeffrey was as tall, dark, and handsome in person as in his photos. I had a margarita but noticed he drank iced tea. I asked him if he ever drank alcohol, although I didn't care either way. Jeffrey said he liked to watch his diet and was very particular about what he put in his body. I respected this but wondered if this guy ever had fun.

Anyway, we talked and laughed for two hours that night. I thought Jeffrey was a decent guy, and when he asked me out for that weekend, I said yes. This is when he told me he was in the process of selling his Dallas home, and would I like to drive to Austin? (Red Flag #2: When something isn't clear in their communication, ask questions. Jeffrey's verbiage led me to believe he had homes in each city with no intention of changing that). I ignored this discrepancy, and I convinced myself that maybe I'd incorrectly read his profile or that he was planning on buying another home in Dallas.

We had a blast that next weekend. I asked my friend, a private investigator, to do a full background check on Jeffrey since I was spending the weekend in another city with a new man, although I had a hotel room for myself, just in case. Jeffrey came back clean. He had no arrest records, he owned his homes, and he seemed to have everything together.

That weekend we went out to dinner, floated on the Comal and Guadalupe Rivers, and basically had more fun than I had had since my breakup a year before. Jeffrey drove me around in his little Mercedes convertible while we listened to country music and Joel Osteen. (Red flags #3 and #4 quickly surfaced, although I didn't see them until later. The car wasn't his, but it belonged to a female friend with whom he also traded house keys. Also, who listens to Joel Osteen on a Saturday night unless you are trying to win over a Christian girl?).

Jeffrey dropped me at the airport Sunday night, kissing me goodbye and telling me he was "smitten." I was flattered, although I giggled to myself that 1975 wants its word back.

Quickly, we fell into the pattern of seeing each other two weekends a month and some weekdays when it worked. Jeffrey would drive to Dallas, or I would make the trek to Austin. The weekends in between our times together were work weekends for him since he was the co-owner and CEO of a tech company, or so he told me.

When we weren't together physically, I would wait for him to call or text. If I didn't answer right away, I knew I might miss his call that day. Whenever I called him, my call went directly to voicemail. (Red Flag #5: When someone sends you to voicemail automatically, every single time, they have something else going on, no doubt). I complained about this to Jeffrey, but nothing changed. He just questioned me with, "Don't you understand how hard I am working? I am the founder of a company with multimillion-dollar potential for me alone."

Eight months later, I was in Austin at his home and my unthinkable happened. One morning, I noticed some Red Bull drinks and a new bottle of tequila on the counter. Those hadn't been there a week ago! I knew Jeffrey didn't touch this stuff because his body was his temple (Red flag #6: Many people who are self-absorbed and perhaps a bit narcissistic are obsessed with their bodies. They put how they look over everything else). Jeffrey was the type to make his own juice; drink fresh, unpasteurized milk; and stock my fridge with his own groceries. My stomach turned over at the thought of someone else being at his home, but I didn't say anything.

Later that evening, we were cooking shrimp and making a salad for dinner. Jeffrey began unloading the dishwasher, so I pitched in. He was talking so much he didn't notice when I pulled out two champagne glasses, followed by a wine glass, and two plates. (Red flag #6: Why two champagne flutes? Who had been over here?) I grew sick to my stomach again. I quickly said a silent prayer, asking for God to show me a sign if this guy was cheating on me. The hairs on the back of my neck and my gut were certainly telling me that this wasn't an honest man.

Right before bed, I discovered my toothpaste and shampoo had been moved to the guest bathroom from the drawer I used in his bathroom. (Red Flag #7: Who was he hiding my things from?) I was a wreck, but I was working on my histrionics, because I can jump to conclusions faster than my dog chases a squirrel. I told myself to sit with my uncomfortable feelings, but I didn't sleep at all that night.

The next day I tried to act normal until I drove back to Dallas. I was headed out around 5 p.m., and for the first time, Jeffrey seemed anxious for me to leave. He told me to call him when I got home because he would be packing for a trip to Boston the next day. Business was booming, he said, and these clients in Massachusetts wanted to meet the CEO.

At 8 p.m., as soon as I returned home, I called Jeffrey. His phone rang once and went to voicemail. I then texted him and said, "Hi, Babe. Thanks for a great weekend. I miss you already." I got no response that night. I was sick. I knew, in my gut, he was with another woman. I cried all night.

One thing I hadn't told him was that I had a good friend who lived in his neighborhood. Late the next morning, I called Lisa and asked her to check his house. Was he home? Was his garage door shut or open? He was supposed to be traveling, but something told me he wasn't.

Around noon, Lisa sent me a picture of his open garage door, with the little Mercedes inside. However, there was a white Tesla parked in my spot. Jeffrey wasn't on a work trip.

I knew I had to end it, even when he responded to my Sunday text eighteen hours later. He wrote, "I am dreaming about our great weekend together." It's okay for you to throw up in your mouth. I did.

I let his response sit for an hour, then I wrote, "I am dreaming about my freedom. I am done. Best of luck to you."

It took him another six hours to respond to me, asking me to rethink my decision. He said he would be home from Boston that weekend and would drive straight to Dallas. I just needed to let him know when I wanted him there. Boston does rhyme with Austin, but bottom line was he was a liar and a cheater.

Um . . . no. I never responded.

Later that year, my friend Holly did some research and couldn't find a record of Jeffrey being a CEO anywhere. He wasn't even listed on the website of the company where he'd said he worked. His social media was locked down, so he didn't leave a trail to follow. My guess is Jeffrey wasn't traveling for work those weekends. Jeffrey was seeing other women either in Dallas, Austin, or Miami, another favorite destination. And like me, I bet they thought their relationships with him were exclusive.

After the shock and pain of the breakup faded, I could look at the lessons I'd learned from this. Of course, they are in this book, but here's a main one: We need to date smart. We need to be nonjudgmental and wait for the other person to show us who they really are. I call this being a heartbreaker and not being heart broken. We can't expect others to treat us the way we treat them. We are often meeting strangers or acquaintances, and they have had entire lives before we came in the picture. Watch, wait, and then decide if they are worth your time.

Is Dating Today a S*#t Show?

Although my story about Jeffrey is an example of a man without character, dating isn't always a painful mess. If we take every date's actions personally and focus too much on the end game, we will guarantee ourselves suffering. We can't let others, especially a stranger from a dating app, determine our value. We must develop healthy skills and mindsets before taking this journey to find love. When we gain that confidence and understanding, we can navigate the ups and downs without getting hurt. Modern dating can be a fantastic journey to understanding ourselves while finding the love of our lives.

We can't let others, especially a stranger from a dating app, determine our value.

Divorce statistics show almost 50 percent of marriages in the United States will end in divorce, while that number jumps to 60 percent and 73 percent for second and third marriages, respectively.[3] That means a large percentage of people have gone through one or several marriages or serious relationships, and I am guessing most of us didn't expect to find ourselves braving this roller coaster ride once again. We thought we had found love, then it was gone. Dating again can feel like a roller coaster with its difficulties, sudden turns, and rapid stops. We can't anticipate when someone will ghost us, misrepresent themselves, or break our heart. We can end up choosing the wrong person just so we can get off this crazy amusement park ride.

Several years ago, I was right where you may be. I used to go on a date and if the guy didn't ask me out at the end of it for a second meeting (even if I didn't like him), I would take it to heart and blame myself. I would tell myself, "Laura, you must be a loser and hard to love." My automatic inner critic would also say to me, "You are worthless." These voices in my head were loud, and the feelings from hearing them were devastating. Any date would end in in despair if someone ghosted or cancelled on me. I even blamed myself when there was no chemistry! Can you imagine what happened when a guy stood me up for a fourth date? I sank into a puddle of tears on my kitchen floor. (That story is ahead, too.)

Granted, my reactions of misery and hopelessness were rooted in more than just disappointment from mediocre dating experiences. My experiences in childhood coupled with a long-term toxic partner played a huge role in the emotional discord resulting from dating, even after years of therapy. The lesson here is that we can all be triggered by dating, and it takes some special guidance for you to navigate this new world without losing your heart, sanity, and soul. We dissect dating and emotions throughout this book.

I've been, by choice, single for seven years. I have had three long-term relationships in between single seasons, and I fell in love with two of those men. In this dating world, I have seen it all or something remarkably close. I've had hundreds of dates, and I've developed an algorithm for dating wherein you use the experience as an opportunity for growth, wisdom, discernment, persistence, patience, and finally, recognition when the love of your life walks through the door.

As I author this book, I am dating someone special. Each day I learn something new about him that brings me closer and more at peace with being in a solid relationship.

All of this is to say, I am going to be real and raw about dating. You need to know what's out there, so welcome to reality. That's where we will begin. If anyone tells you that they love dating because it's all unicorns and rainbows, they are either having mind-blowing sex with each person they go out with, or they are smoking something strong and likely illegal. There are good people, bad people, broken people, healed people, abusive people, kind people, and many other types out there to date. If you expect to always find Disneyland and Mickey Mouse, you're setting yourself up for sorrow and misery. The truth is you may find yourself in a junkyard, face-to-face with a rat.

I feel like I need to give you examples of some things you may come across that may turn you off dating apps. For every Mickey Mouse, there is a rat. Recently, and not by choice, I've had three *couples* swipe right (that's yes) on me on Bumble, their profiles saying they want to bring some spice to their relationship. Um . . . NO. I laughed, thought about how broken their relationship must really be, and swiped left (that's a hard no.) Just be prepared. Nothing is off-limits for some people, although most apps let you report things you find disturbing.

In this book, I am going to teach you how to stop taking things personally. From this point forward, there will be no "zero" expectations, no love clouds or rose-tinted goggles, and no emotional crashes. I am going to give you the power to go on date after date and enjoy the ride without getting your heart broken.

I am going to give you the power to go on date after date and enjoy the ride without getting your heart broken.

It's taken me a lot of work to get where I am now. I can go on a date that doesn't work out (for whatever reason), tell them thank you, and go about my life without hard feelings or despair. Sometimes the dates are even hilarious! I can date multiple people, so I don't get focused on the *one* guy. No, I am not intimate with all or even a few of them. For me, sex comes with a committed relationship and a promise of a solid future. (Yes, we will talk about sex, too.)

Also, I can have conversations with men that are really interviews, but they have no idea I am moving down my checklist. I'll teach you this tactic, because whether you are a man or woman, it can protect you. I am not vulnerable until I know a person is a safe person. They must deserve to know the innermost and personal details of my life. And finally, when a man is rude or condescending, I can walk out the door of a restaurant without looking back and speaking to him ever again. That my friends, is self-confidence and power. You can get there, too.

Your authority and self-esteem will grow exponentially from reading this book. I am here to hold your hand and help you every step of the way. My friend Amy often says, "Don't play a player!" Amy also likes to say, "Keep it moving." She is correct, and I am going to teach you how, so hang on tight. We will change how you date so one day that special person says, "Stop!" to your heart, mind, and soul. And you will be whole and happy when they do.

The Four Main Things You Will Learn from Me Are:

1. You can't and won't take it personally. No one else will determine your value but you.

2. You will be the best version of you while you date, from your character to your appearance. You don't need to change for anyone. You are authentically you.

3. Fast in means fast out. You must slow down in every aspect of dating.

4. Red flags are red flags. Run.

Don't rush into dating until you've read this book in its entirety. It can prepare you for the wild ride. You will be a heart breaker, not heartbroken, because you'll be armed with knowledge many others don't have. You won't be grasping at the first decent date because you "need" companionship. Get a dog for that. You deserve a relationship and true, unconditional love. You deserve to find the love of your life. Let's go.

CHAPTER 2

UNDERSTANDING THE GOOD, BAD, AND UGLY ABOUT DATING

DATING STORY #2

Dog Pee and the Twenty-Dollar Man

This is the story of how I ended up with twenty dollars less in my pocket than when I started and dog pee in my house.

Several years ago, I connected with a guy named Rich on a dating app. We decided to meet for margaritas at my favorite place that evening. He mentioned that he had a black lab, named Harley, that he didn't want to leave in the back of his brand-new pickup, because the dog might jump out and cruise the parking lot.

No worries, I told him. I can stick Harley in my back yard for you and come right back. (I didn't want him to know where I lived. But I didn't mind his dog, or so I thought, because I love dogs.) I brought Harley home, and since this guy said the dog was housetrained, I put him inside with my cocker spaniel, Paris. It wasn't love at first sight, but they seemed to get along, so I gave them each a treat and told them to be good.

Rich and I had a nice time over drinks, and when the bill came, Rich said he had no money due to his truck payment. I cringed but offered to pay the bill anyway. Oh, and I must add, Rich carried a strong aura of thick cigarette smoke. It was like a cloud followed him, although his profile said he didn't smoke.

Anyway, I said he could follow me to get his dog because he seemed like a nice guy and had already checked out on my background check. When we walked in to get Harley, the first thing I noticed and smelled was dog pee. Harley had marked every corner of my sofa, chairs, and kitchen table legs as his territory. Rich didn't seem to notice, so I just shuttled the dog and his smokey owner out the door as quickly as possible. I didn't return any subsequent calls.

Lesson Learned: Don't bring your dog as a wingman unless it's an outdoor bar that allows them. Even then, ask your date if it's ok. Also, have at least twenty dollars in your pocket or a credit card if you've offered to buy her a drink. It cost me twenty dollars at the restaurant and then five times that to clean my carpets and furniture. Harley was a sweet dog, but his owner needed a lesson on thoughtfulness. My lesson? Never offer to do anything that puts you out or makes you uncomfortable, even if it involves your favorite animal.

The Good About Dating

1. You know what you want.

By now, you likely know what you want out of a relationship, and you just need to learn how to acquire it. Let's start with a basic expectation: most people want either a casual relationship or a long-term relationship. There's a big difference.

A casual relationship means just that: casual. There is no commitment. You are both free to date other people. Many times, this also means there is no anticipatory communication or dating schedule or standard. You may see this person on a Friday night but not hear from them until the next Wednesday.

The casual aspect also applies to sex. You may have sex with this person but being intimate doesn't mean you are in a committed relationship with them. You both are free to have sex with other people without disclosing it to each other. In my experience, I find that men are more likely to want a casual relationship, particularly if they have left a long partnership or marriage. As a woman, I can say that many women prefer a long-term relationship and eventually struggle with being with someone casually.

Long-term relationships (LTR) are when two people meet and want to build something lasting with the other. The goals for many people, but not all, in long-term relationships are monogamy and building a life together. There are expectations around communication, dates, sex, children, and money. People who want a LTR often want true love, companionship, exclusivity, and more.

Many dating apps offer users the choice to say if they are searching for a casual or long-term relationship. Whatever that person says, believe it. Don't date the guy who says he wants casual because you plan to change his mind. This goes for women, too. If any woman says they want casual, they are looking for no-strings-attached dates and sex. Either way, these people don't want the responsibilities that come with a committed relationship. I don't care if you look like Beyonce or Josh Lucas; you won't change someone's mind that wants "casual." I know sixty-year-old men that have never been married and still desire "casual," no matter how smart, beautiful, and kind a woman is.

Don't date the guy who says he wants casual because you plan to change his mind.

Also, if you want casual, please don't overlook the "LTR" label. Have integrity and don't deceive long-term relationship seekers by letting them think you want exclusivity. People who want casual relationships have certain needs, and people who want long-term commitments have their desires, too. Trust the process. Be real. Be honest. Be true to yourself and others. I believe in karma. When you don't respect someone's wishes and go with deception instead, it will come back to bite you.

2. It's easy to meet people online

Another reason dating is easier now than in the past is the number of dating apps and websites from which you can choose. These offer the typical user a variety of dating communities in which you can meet or swipe on hundreds of people a day. Here are some of the most popular sites, most of which have apps now, too.

Bumble

Tinder

Match

Elite Singles

Farmers Only

Zoosk

Think about the math. If you were to go into a bar, restaurant, or church group tonight, you might meet one or two people in three hours. Chances are these new acquaintances wouldn't be what you are searching for. However, on a dating site, you can swipe on sixty people in three minutes. This increases the odds that you will meet someone with whom you have a connection.

You can do background checks or look at a potential date's social media.

Social media can be a blessing or a curse, but when it comes to dating, it's a huge gift. If you want to peep into someone's life, even if it's their highlight reel, you can check out their social media. For example, maybe you don't want to date someone with kids, but then you see on their Instagram story they have seven children. There's your answer. It's time to move on. Or maybe you want to date a person who is active and loves the outdoors. When you look them up on Facebook, their profile picture is of them climbing a mountain. You now know you're more likely to be a match.

Also, there are many websites and services that offer background checks for a minimal fee. You can learn almost everything about someone over the last twenty years of their life. A client of mine did a background search on a potential partner, and she found that he didn't really own the car he was driving. However, he did own the house he lived in. She also learned this man had two speeding tickets and a DUI. To her, these weren't huge red flags, but it did lessen her desire to be in a committed relationship with this person.

I recommend before you go on a first date, do your own investigation. You can pay a small fee and do a background check on a website like https://truthfinder.com or https://beenverified.com. You can also hire a private investigator to run a background check for you for a larger fee. These investigations are thorough, providing details such as where your date has lived and been employed over the last twenty years. These background checks also specify any marriages or children the person may have. I wouldn't recommend using the more expensive version until you are more serious about someone. However, I would never advise skipping on doing a full background check if you are thinking of being engaged to someone or living with them.

There are, however, some things you cannot find out through background checks, no matter how thorough. This is where you use your instinct. For example, I had a friend during my years in television named April. April was a producer who was smart and funny, and she didn't want any nonsense, especially in dating.

April decided to use her contacts and asked her police buddy in this small Texas town to run background checks on her dates. One guy, Jay, looked great on paper, yet April was concerned he was lying about loving cats as much as she did. When she learned his apartment didn't allow pets, she knew he wasn't telling the truth. It turned out that the guy didn't own a cat but borrowed one as needed from a friend, and the feline wanted nothing to do with Jay. From that day on, we called Jay "rent-a-cat." This was funny and sad at the same time. Background checks are important, yet so is your intuition.

1. Online dating no longer has the stigma it had years ago.

There was a time online dating seemed illicit or shady. Now, almost everyone who is dating uses a site or app. The associated shame no longer exists. Some figures show that three hundred million people worldwide use online dating sites.[4] Anecdotally, I have been to many weddings where the pastor joked that God worked through Bumble or Match.com to bring the couple together.

Also, online dating allows for you to date in many different communities. You can date people from all over the world or within different zip codes near your home. You can date people of various ethnicities or ages. You can choose to meet a professional, an entrepreneur, a retired person, a factory worker, a government employee, or a stay-at-home mom or dad. The choice of whom to meet is yours.

2. There are coaches and therapists who can help you date.

Many people who have navigated the dating scene, or counsel clients who are dating, can also offer help. I am giving you many of my secrets as a dating coach, but there is always an extra boost when you have a person cheering you on while dating. My therapist, a man, often gives me dating advice from a male perspective. He tells me when I am being overreactive (I am good at that) or when I need to cut bait and run. This counselor also helps me listen to my inner voice and discern what it is telling me to do.

I have also used someone who is a coach and matchmaker, but I feel like I should've asked more questions before saying yes to her offered services. This person is skilled at what she does, but we aren't a match in communication styles. When you are an empath like me, and thus extremely sensitive, you need someone who can give you the truth with love. This woman gave me the truth but didn't understand that I sometimes came from a place of doubt. She didn't comprehend why I'd asked the question in the first place. We all need the truth, but some people react to the ways in which the messages are relayed. That said, a dating coach or matchmaker can help, but make sure your communication styles, values, and morals match.

I am a coach who gives my clients the truth in a way that builds them up and doesn't minimize their wishes or chip away at their confidence. I am a Christian, yet don't live by the adage that you must date a certain way to find the person of your dreams. You need to date like you. You do not need to change your character, appearance, values, and morals to attract the "right" man or woman. Everyone has different wants and needs when dating, and I am here to listen to those and support my clients. I am my clients' biggest cheerleader.

The Bad

Let's flip the script and look at the downsides of dating today, especially in the online world.

1. Online dating gives the perception of so many choices.

When I first started dating online after my divorce, I asked a good guy friend to tell me about dating via apps or websites. Mark described it as shopping in a candy store. He referred to hundreds or thousands of women on some sites for others to see and possibly match with. Granted, Mark met the love of his life on eHarmony.com., so it does work!

Anyway, the candy store is what many people want after a divorce, and this is where trouble can start. It's a double-edged sword. There are so many people to swipe on that the number of profiles give the illusion that there is always something better out there. It happens every day. People meet someone online and exchange a few texts, then one party goes silent or disappears altogether. I have talked to both men and women who have experienced this with online dating. Dating apps make it easier to have zero accountability or offer no explanation.

Also, for those in relationships, the vast numbers of online dating users make it seem if one relationship doesn't work out, there's another just around the corner. Maybe, or maybe not. I believe there are only a handful of people with whom you'll will have a true, solid, loving connection. We need to hold onto these people. Unconditional love doesn't come around every day.

> I believe there are only a handful of people with whom you'll have a true, solid, loving connection. We need to hold onto these people.

Think about the chemistry you may or may not feel with someone. Chemistry is rare. Perhaps you've been on a hundred dates. Chances are that you will feel butterflies and serious attraction with one of those dates. One. That's one percent of your effort. This is where some people make the mistake of keeping on looking for other options when the treasure is right in front of them.

Here's another learning point for you: You can't change that such people think the grass next door is greener. It's not your fault they will find a brown and crunchy yard after you. It's their loss. You will likely be married or in a solid relationship before they have a second date with a potential partner. Someone will see your greatness and want to water it for the rest of their lives. Be patient, and be aware that these flakey, indecisive people exist. It's not about you.

2. It's easy to ghost or disappear.

Ghosting means the practice of ending a personal relationship with someone by suddenly and without explanation withdrawing from all communication. Almost everyone who dates these days may have this happen. I have. Why? Online dating and other avenues of technology have made it easy to simply disappear. There have been men that I corresponded with for several days via an app, and then these people suddenly took down their profile. They give no explanation. For all I know they are dead, although I think even if someone died, their profile would stay up for a few days or weeks! I don't mean to be dark, but ghosting can be ridiculous.

I also find that people are more likely to have someone ghost them after they exchange last names. For example, I messaged with a guy on an app who lived five miles away from me. He seemed kind, intelligent, and smart.

We exchanged last names, and he asked for my number—then boom! He disappeared. I have had this happen a few times. People can be very judgmental, and they see that I am an author and have helped thousands of people through narcissistic abuse with books and videos. This scares some men, I think. Instead of behaving like a human being and asking questions, they run.

One afternoon, after this happened on an online dating app, I told a friend that maybe I was too much for the concerned guy. She said, "No, Laura. Maybe he's not enough for you." Now, after some reflection, I agree. I write to help people leave toxic relationships and find love. Maybe he was scared because he was a narcissist or because he couldn't handle the small amount of attention I've had. I don't know. But he showed me he's not the one for me. I require someone that supports me emotionally, yet calls me out when I am making a mistake. I don't want a coward who can't even text to say he's going in a different direction. If this has happened to you, I hope you see where the character flaw lies. And it's not with you.

There is someone for everyone. Don't let the ghosts ruin it for you.

You may message with someone and exchange names, and this person thinks you're the best thing since ice cream. You just don't know. When the time is right, give them your last name. I've had men do the opposite and want to date me long distance, and I mean thousands of miles away. There is someone for everyone. Don't let the ghosts ruin it for you.

3. People can mispresent themselves.

You may think you've met the person of your dreams, then you meet in person, and you feel defeated. That's why I shared my dating story about Greg. You haven't done anything wrong. Some people are just fakers because they feel like they can't get a date being honest about themselves. You'll see profiles where people use pictures of different people or describe themselves as having a life of which they can only dream. Again, this is where background checks come in handy. Later in the book, I'll talk about further investigative steps to take when you become serious with someone.

4. Some people put their pain from past relationships on you.

So many people walk around with the pain of every past unsuccessful relationship heavily weighing them down. These people are either afraid of confronting their part in a relationship's disintegration, or they feel like they have done nothing wrong. Either way is not good. Someone who really wants to be with you will work on their side of things. They will work on themselves. You can't have one whole if two halves are broken.

Asking someone to get therapy isn't something you do on a first date, but if you're heading into the love boat, you need to discuss it. We will talk about this when we discuss getting serious with someone.

5. Timing is everything.

Timing is everything. We've heard that thousands of times when it comes to relationships, job opportunities, pregnancy, or whatever the end goal is. And yes, it's true—especially with relationships.

I met a great man once who still felt broken from his divorce ten years earlier. He was doing everything he could to get better: therapy, coaching, books, videos, podcasts, and more. I would've have dated him in a heartbeat. His love for God, his family, and friends had knocked me off my feet. He was a successful businessman, yet humility was his middle name. But he wasn't ready for a relationship. He was still mourning the past. I hope he will be healed one day and be a great husband for someone. But for me? The timing wasn't right. Even if we'd dated, the broken parts would have taken over and it wouldn't have worked. With people like this, you don't want to waste your time. Time is such a precious commodity that it's important to spend it where there's value and potential. Again, would this be about you? No. No one can make someone ready for a relationship until they do the work.

6. Monitor your love cloud and red flags.

We are so connected via technology that's it's easy to want constant contact. That's not healthy for a relationship at any given point. If we aren't careful while we are dating, every phone call, text, or lack thereof can send us into a joyful, emotionally charged daydream or a downward spiral. When we base our worth, self-esteem, and self-confidence on what others think, especially potential partners or lovers, we are setting ourselves up for failure.

Here's the catch. Like my former life coach, Rebecca Lynn Pope, often told me, "Laura, come down off your love cloud so you can see what is right in front of you." (Ya'll, I am so good at living on a love cloud. It's fun up there! But the fall out of the sky isn't worth it.) If you don't come down off your cloud and take off your love goggles, you will eventually plummet to the ground with a painful landing.

Red Flags don't change color.

Red flags don't change color. If you're on your love cloud, you won't see them. Don't climb that high. Be realistic. We are dealing with human beings, and humans are flawed creatures. Keep your feet on the ground so you can see what's in front of you. Again, the red flags aren't because of you, nor can you change their color. But you can see them for what they are. That's your boundary and responsibility.

Negative and Positive Character Traits of those in the Dating World

Below, I have described the negative and positive character traits of people. For the most part, you cannot change someone's character. If something in this list doesn't work for you when you meet a potential date or friend, move on. Let's start with the negative traits so we can end on a positive note.

People can have these negative character traits. The best internal response for you is given in parentheses.

- **Flakey** – You converse with an interest on a dating site for days, then they just disappear. Their profile is gone, or they stop responding to messages, even if you ask, "Are you okay?"

  (*Move on. You don't want flakey people because they don't change. Do you want to be in the delivery room while the father is at a bar watching college football? Or do you want your partner to go MIA when it's time to pay the house payment? No loss here.*)

- **Judgmental** – They have four kids by four baby daddies or mommies, yet they tell you that you have issues because you communicate with your ex on email only.

  (*Forget it. They need a major lesson in boundaries and healthy relationships. It's not your job to teach them because it might take years.*)

- **Broken** – They were abused and abandoned as children, so they sabotage the best relationships because that's all they know how to do. You are a catch, but they can't see that because pain distorts their vision.

  (*You will exhaust yourself trying to convince them how amazing you are. Realize that yourself and move on.*)

- **Unwilling to heal** – Healing seems like too much work, so these people just date person after person with similar issues. It's like putting a Band-Aid on each wound instead of allowing each cut to heal. Pain is layered on top of pain. Then they project their anguish and despair on you. Perhaps their ex-wife or ex-husband was unfaithful, and you've never cheated in your life. It won't matter. You're labeled a cheater because of the damage they suffered at the hands of others months or years ago.

  (*Bless the heart of the person who ends up with this guy or gal. They will never escape the accusations and blame shifting. Run, friend, run!*)

- **Skilled at projecting** – These people use a mental process by which they attribute to others what is in their own minds, i.e., "Why are you so angry all the time?" This can also happen when one partner is cheating on the other. The unfaithful person berates the innocent partner for even glancing at another person in the grocery store.

  (*Walk or run away. These people don't take responsibility for anything they are doing wrong.*)

- **Sad** – Some people are clinically depressed and have no business dating. They need help from a therapist and a psychiatrist first. But it's easier for them to try to find someone else to fix their sadness. "You make me happy," they say. That's a lot of pressure to put on someone else.

  (*I dated someone with untreated clinical depression. In 2020, the NIH said 8.4 percent of Americans had a major depressive episode. It's treatable with medicine and therapy. When it's not under control, depression can cause detachment and loneliness, both of which put a strain on relationships. You can't fix these people, either. They must want help. Move on.*)

- **Angry** – These people have an underlying sense of rage almost all the time. They could be narcissists, but regardless, they seem consistently angry and seldom happy.

  (*Anger can lead to lasting scars in the target and relationship. Think about what this could lead to. There's a chance of psychological, emotional, or physical abuse of you or other family members, including your kids. You deserve more.*)

- **Bitter** – These people have been burned by a relationship with a parent, sibling, partner, child, colleague, or friend. They won't seek help to get better, so their resentment and cynicism permeates their daily life. They may blame you for their problems.

(These people resemble those carrying around a lot of anger. Bitter people ruin relationships at home and work. No one likes being around them. Don't try to save them because only therapy can do that. You will walk on eggshells the rest of your life if you stay unless they get help.)

- **Playing the field** – These people rarely settle down because "the grass is always greener." Often, they look at women or men as objects or possessions to be used as they deem necessary. These types of people only settle down if they face a health or monetary crisis and need your assistance. These are people you date that tell you, "My last relationship was with someone twenty years younger than you. They could have sex for hours and looked amazing."

  (Please. *Put your wall up emotionally when you get the vibe that they are a player. You cannot change them. I have met seventy-five-year-old men and women that are still players.)*

- **Wanting only sex** – They want to experience sex with as many people as possible. These "players" will date and be intimate with the young, old, married, divorced, widowed . . . the list goes on. Sometimes these people turn out to be bi-sexual because they cannot get enough.

  (If this is for you, great. Be careful and use protection. If not, you dodge a bullet by saying no to this type of person. You've also said no to contracting a sexually transmitted disease and being needed solely for your ability to be a sexual release for them. No, thank you. This isn't a transaction. Emotions are involved. Goodbye!)

- **Collecting phone numbers** – Some people on dating apps will converse for a few days, then ask for your number. Then they'll disappear and never call or text. You may be left feeling like you told them a secret that they didn't appreciate. No, sweetheart, they just wanted your number.

(If collecting numbers helps them feel better about themselves, then we have a bigger problem at hand: low self-esteem and zero confidence. You would be their greatest cheerleader with no halftime. Ever.)

- **Liars** – People lie, but some in the dating world take it to new heights. Their lies have just enough truth in them that you think they are telling the truth. I dated a man once who said he was part owner in a tech company. It turns out he wasn't even listed as an employee on the company's website. He drove a fast little Mercedes convertible that I thought belonged to him, yet after an easy, online background check, I learned it was registered to a neighbor he was close friends with. A female neighbor. So many red flags here.

  (If something seems fishy, it probably is. Do your background checks through a private investigator or one of the many websites online. Don't be duped by the charmers and chameleons out there. You don't want that! You never know what you'll come home to.)

- **Cheaters** – These people fall in the category of liars, too, because you must spin a strong, complicated web of lies to get away with multiple partners. For example, a friend of mine years ago found out the married man she was sleeping with also had a girlfriend and a "friend" at work. She was devastated this guy was cheating on her. Gently and firmly, I explained to her that he was cheating on all *four* of them.

  (Nothing good comes from dating a person who is a cheater. If this person cheated with you, who says he or she won't be unfaithful to you? It's not always the case, but if a person has cheated multiple times, then there's a pattern. In patterns we find truths. Bye bye, boy or girl.)

- **Living with Mom** – I've added this to my dating checklist that you will find in an upcoming chapter. Ask where a potential partner lives, or do a background check. At one point, a guy I had been on several dates with asked if I could Uber to his house and pick him up. Charles wasn't ready, so I walked down the hall to wait. There's was a room with a quilt and knickknacks everywhere. Guess what? Charles lived with his mom.

Another boyfriend lost his high paying job while we were dating and moved in with his mother. It was obvious she was paying the rent. They enjoyed having coffee together every morning and watching the news. After six months of no employment, the strain was too much on the relationship. We broke up.

(Great people can find themselves in tough financial situations. There's nothing wrong with living with Mom or Dad, but watch to see if it's permanent. Is it their work ethic or simply hard knocks? You don't want to carry the financial burden of the entire relationship unless you can easily do that and think the person is worth it.)

- **Posturing** – There are people who will present an entirely different persona to you than what they are. I am a woman of faith, and most men learn that quickly. I typically ask on the second or third date what church they go to. Most dates have an answer to that. However, when I ask them to remind me who the pastor is at that church, they often stutter. They don't know because they don't really go. For me, it's not the fact that a man doesn't attend a church regularly that's the deal-breaker. I want to tell them, "Just don't lie about it." If you're a sales rep, say you're a sales rep. Don't tell me you are the CEO of the company. I will find out what the truth is, and after this book, you'll get to the truth quickly, too.

(Posturing makes my gag reflex kick in. Why people put on airs and pretend to be something they aren't baffles me. I would rather have you be you. Authenticity is attractive. Look for someone real who is likely around the corner.)

- **Standing you up** – You spend the time to get ready for a date. You look and smell nice, and you take the time to drive to the designated place. You wait and you wait. And they don't show up. Of course, you

THE NEW TRUTH ABOUT DATING

text to make sure everything is ok, and you don't get a response. They aren't coming. They stood you up. This has happened to me on a fourth date. Don't tolerate it. If they call or text later, don't respond. Move on. Unless they are in the hospital after a terrible accident or their child or parent just died, there is no excuse for their behavior, since their phone still works.

(Unless someone's parent, child, or favorite pet died, or they are in the hospital, there is no reason to stand their date up. Ever. My best friend had a date that had a motorcycle accident and ended up in the hospital. He called her from Presbyterian's ER with a concussion and broken leg. The date should either call or text if they cannot make it. It's ridiculous if they don't. No skin lost in this game. Keep going.)

- **Ghosting you** - Ghosting is a dating term that refers to abruptly cutting off contact with someone without giving that person any warning or explanation. Even when the person being ghosted reaches out to reinitiate contact or gain closure, they're met with silence. Recently, people have learned to send read receipts to show the sender their message has been read and opened. "I've put them on "read,"" people say. This means I let the other person know that I read their message, and I didn't respond. The message to the person is, "You aren't important enough for me to even respond to your text." It's rude, but when someone conveniently exits and enters your life at their convenience, this iPhone feature is convenient, too.

(Like Greg in my dating story, the only reason to ghost is rudeness, meanness, or harassment. If someone is jacked up when you break it off with them, then disappear. You may be able to be friends one day, but not right now. It's not worth it. Also, if you've been the nice person that I know you are, and someone ghosts you, you win. They have no character or integrity. Next, please.)

Positive character traits:

- **Loving** – There are people who love their families, friends, and eventually, you. They are excited to be around you and introduce you to those who are closest to them and mean the most to them.

  (If this happens, they really like you. Enjoy taking this big step while learning more about the person you're with.)

- **Kind** – There are men and women who are the nicest people you will meet. One man brought chocolate milk to my son during Covid. A friend of mine had emergency surgery, and a woman he had been on only a few dates with him dropped off food for a week. Others volunteer to help the homeless, mentor young kids, drop off holiday toys to kids who otherwise wouldn't have them, and more.

  (Winner winner chicken dinner on the kindness front. Doesn't mean you must fall for kind people, but true kindness and generosity is a big plus!)

- **Loves animals** –Some of the best advice I ever received from a friend was this: "Watch how a potential love interest treats his mother, animals, and people who can do nothing for him." Many people love their animals almost as much as they love their kids. They hate to see anyone or anything suffer. Men who take care of their moms show compassion, love, and commitment. And those people who treat servers, store clerks, bus boys, flight attendants, and gate agents with respect are people with integrity.

  (Sometimes dogs and cats can tell us all we need to know about a person. If your animal loves your potential partner, then that's a good sign. If your boo loves your animals, even better. Fur trumps a jerk every time. But fur and a good person can mix.)

- **Self-deprecating** – There are men and women who joke about their idiosyncrasies. For example, a friend of mine cannot sing. I mean he can't even come near the correct note. It's so bad, he was kicked out of the school and church choir as a kid. He loves to share that story. I find humor like that delightful. Be sure the person doesn't use it as a "look at me" or "woe is me" trick. But most of the time, self-deprecation shows that someone is human.

(*I love it when people make fun of themselves. I didn't mean to be self-deprecating when I asked the guy I am dating to give me the slowest, biggest, oldest horse when I was on a horseback ride. I had recently seen Jill, a good friend, almost get bucked off a spooked mare. For some reason, my guy was howling at my description of the desired animal. I fear crazy horses like Jill had. I don't want to break a bone. I want to live. That's all. My admission of my fear showed I was human, and that's attractive.*)

- **Intelligent** – While dating, you will have the opportunity to meet some of the smartest people you've ever met. There are men and women who have earned two PhDs, become a record producer for the top talent in Nashville, written screen plays for Hollywood, are able solve the most difficult math problems in the world, and the list goes on. I have a few friends who are brain surgeons. They are brilliant yet humble. The world is wide open for you to meet people like this.

(*Years ago, I was intimidated by a brain surgeon I met in the elevator at a hospital. I asked him what type of doctor he was. He moved his long white coat over and said, "A pediatric brain surgeon. I just got out of surgery where I saved a boy's life." He asked me about my day. Here I was, this blonde drug rep toting her samples and literature, so I was honest. "I dropped off my son at day care, then carried these samples to an office who didn't want them." He laughed. We met for dinner years later, after I was divorced, because we matched on Bumble! Guess what? He's human, funny, and asked great questions. There are so many intelligent people to meet.*)

- **Beautiful**– These people are or were supermodels. You have a chance to meet them. Some are as beautiful on the inside as they are on the outside. Others have a beauty that emanates from deep within, and you find yourself soaking up their presence. You can almost touch how lovely their soul is by their energy they happily share with others.

(*Psychology research done in 2020 shows that people, overall, tend to rate themselves as more physically attractive than strangers rate them. However, it seems that not everyone overestimates their attractiveness to an equal degree.[5] This research, done by researchers at an Austrian University, were initially looking at how unattractive people underestimate their unattractiveness. Sad, I know, that this was even debatable. But the point is, attractive people are easy to find on dating apps. And they have many, many choices because everyone swipes right on them. I personally don't want to be in line to meet them. If there are any words of advice I can give you about this, it's to date up and down. Date all kinds of people. Often people hate online dating because they swipe right on only the pretty people without a response. Give the average person a shot. They may turn out to be the most beautiful person you've ever met because if what's inside. Change the tactic. Find the diamond in the rough. It is SO worth it.*)

- **Funny** – There are actors, clowns, teachers, artists, musicians, and others who are just downright hilarious. People can't keep a straight face around them because they find humor in almost anything. These people are refreshing with their positive outlook on life.

  (*Having a sense of humor can go far in your quest to find the love of your life. Use it!*)

- **Trustworthy** – You will meet people who will hold a secret you tell them in confidence forever. Nothing is shared without permission.

  (*Give this back to that person. Don't tell white lies about being interested when you're not. I've been called out on this before, and it's not something I am proud about. Don't be that guy or girl. Be THE guy or THE girl who does it right.*)

- **Authentic** – You will meet people who say what they mean and mean what they say. It's uplifting. Actions speak louder than words, and for these people with integrity, actions match the verbiage they use.

  (*Be yourself because you want someone to love you just the way you are. Put your best foot forward, but don't change you.*)

- **Wanting a LTR (long-term relationship)** – You will meet people who want a long-term relationship. Some may want it more than you, or you aren't really interested in them at all, but these men and women exist.

  (**Enough said**. He or she is out there.)

- **Affluent** – You will likely meet people who have made or inherited a lot of money. This gives you an opportunity to look at their character and how they treat their success. Do they give to charity? Do they brag about their affluence? Do they have a sense of entitlement that comes with being wealthy?

  (*Money doesn't buy class or happiness. In fact, money can change people for the worse. If they are kind and affluent, then that shows solid character.*)

- **Living on their own** – This is obviously the flip side of the people I dated that live with mom. You'll meet men and women who own their own home or prefer to rent. They have vehicles that are paid off and they carry no debt. This shows responsibility and financial acumen.

  (*Not much more to say about these men and women. Kudos to them for being fiscally responsible. It may be indicative of how they run their lives. Get to know them.*)

A FEW MORE STORIES FROM THE FRONT LINES

DATING STORIES #3 AND #4

Before we conclude our work in Chapter 2, below are a few more stories about dating.

Tesla Man

The Tesla was traveling about eighty-five miles an hour north on Interstate 35 in Dallas. The city lights were a blur through the passenger seat window as I gripped the door handle. My fingers grew numb because my grip was so tight. What had started out as a fun, romantic date had gone sideways. I prayed that I would make it home in one piece.

Before I tell you how this date ended, let me rewind. I had met a man who was the CFO of a hospital system in the Southwest. My job as a pharmaceutical representative has allowed me to meet all kinds of people, from physicians to nurses to chronically ill children. I met Josh when I was calling on one of the pediatric hospitals in Texas.

At first, Josh reminded me of my father. (Dad is a great man, by the way. You'll learn more about him throughout this book). He had red hair like my father and a great laugh. Josh seemed to be a gentleman who checked my boxes, such as asking me out days in advance and calling me rather than texting. In today's dating world, you might receive the equivalent of the Unabomber Manifesto via text before ever getting a short phone call.

Josh and I had our first date in January of 2020 prior to Covid-19, where we met at a nice restaurant and had a glass of wine. I left feeling encouraged. Josh was a great conversationalist, and he said he wouldn't dream of letting me pull out my own chair or pay the bill.

I thought the second date had promise. Josh said to dress up because we would be going downtown. Everything else was a surprise. And was it ever!

He picked me up in his new, hunter-green Tesla. I had never ridden in a car on which the doors flew up like the gates on a Star Wars spaceship.

Once downtown, we headed to a rooftop bar overlooking the city. The weather was beautiful for February, with clear skies, a light breeze, and a temperature of sixty-five degrees. That night, Texas felt like California. I ordered a margarita, my favorite, and he had a beer. Then another. Then another and another and another.

I suggested we head to dinner because it was after eight, and Josh clearly needed some food. He was beginning to talk loudly, and he had become very opinionated. Fortunately, we had parked the car in front of one of the bougiest restaurants in Dallas, so we walked back there for dinner.

Dinner was delicious, enjoyable except for the side show the restaurant's clientele was getting from my date. He had switched to whiskey after his four or five beers, and the more he drank, the louder he became. He was skilled at shoving three rolls in his mouth at one time while telling stories from his childhood so all the restaurant patrons could hear them, too.

Near the end of the date, he began banging his hands on the table to make a point. I remember looking for a side exit so I could slip away and never see this clown again. The people around us were staring, because they knew how to behave at a fine dining establishment. Josh was not the epitome of etiquette.

Let me digress for a minute if you will. For the record, I am more of a Tex-Mex/casual dining kind of girl. Sure, I can enjoy the finest white tablecloth restaurants, but some of the best times and meals I have ever had were at a dive with hamburgers on the grill and cold beer in a giant trough.

Now I'll take you back to the swanky restaurant, where Josh finally needed a bathroom break. This was my chance to motion the server over.

"I am so sorry for the sad circus at our table," I told him. "Please bring us the check."

When Josh returned, the server quickly handed him the check. Josh scribbled his name, and we were out of there to let the other diners eat in peace.

I told Josh I was ordering an Uber because he was in no shape to drive. He told me it was okay because his car would drive us home. I can hear my grandmother saying, "Never in my life . . ."

The car did drive us home. Josh plugged in my address and kept a finger or two on the steering wheel to let the car know he was awake. Apparently, this Tesla model shuts down if a certain amount of time passes without touches from the driver's hands.

After I made it home that evening, around 11 p.m., I thanked Josh and ran into my house.

The next day he sent me a text asking me out again, which I returned with a gentle, "I don't think we're a match, but thank you for asking."

I guess Josh was angry, because my phone then beeped with a Venmo request from him for $250. That was half of the cost of the meal that I didn't want to have in the first place. A Slurpee from 7-11 would have been more enjoyable than that debacle. I deleted the request, then blocked him.

Lesson I learned: When a date starts off with someone intoxicated or unaware of their obtrusive, obnoxious behavior, it's okay to leave. Always be ready to take an Uber, no matter the reason. I should've excused myself to go to the ladies' room and used the kitchen door at the back of the restaurant to escape. I am sure the maître d would have helped me cut and run.

Jace (the good men don't have nicknames)

I had been divorced for a little over a year, and I had immediately dated a man much like my ex. When that went sideways, as all relationships with narcissists do, I took some more time to heal, then jumped onto Bumble.

On Bumble, like many dating apps, the user swipes right for a "yes" and left for a "no." I had swiped left on several profiles for one reason or another, and then this handsome, Christian man named Jace popped up. One of his pictures was with his dog, a huge Golden retriever. His profile was professionally written, and he had four kids. (I find that I match better with men who have children and been married. We have more in common.) I thought to myself that this guy seemed authentic.

I swiped right on him, and Bumble notified us that we were a match. On Bumble, women make the first move, so I sent a message. A few hours later he replied.

We met the next week for dinner at a favorite Tex-Mex joint and closed the restaurant. The servers had to kick us out after closing time. Jace later said he was so attracted to me he wanted to kiss me, but I jumped in my car too quickly and sped off. I was nervous, I guess, because I was attracted to him, too.

Jace and I dated for the next year. He was a consummate gentleman. He would open doors for me, hold my hand, ask me how my day was, and make sure my son was okay. I have learned to not judge men but to let them prove themselves as the relationship unfolds. Jace didn't do one thing that I can remember that hurt my feelings. He wasn't a game player or a "player" like some men in their forties. He was accessible and kind. He didn't try to hurt me or gaslight me as narcissists do. He was my safe place.

Some of my favorite things we did together were to go see live music and take our dogs to the dog park. Jace eventually met my son, and I met his children. My son Carson still asks about him. In teenager speak, "He is a cool dude."

You are likely asking why didn't it work out? I don't want to say much because I don't want to identify him. Just know that if he had taken better care of himself after his divorce and before meeting me, I think we would be married now. I cried and cried when we broke up. Jace was and is a good, good man.

I think of him daily. I hear he's happy, and for that, I am grateful.

Lesson Learned: Let the relationship unfold naturally. Don't get invested too quickly. Watch the actions of the other person and decide if it's something you can live with the rest of your life. There's no rush. When it's right, it's easy.

CHAPTER 3

DATING AFTER A BREAKUP OR TOXIC RELATIONSHIP

There's a reason you bought this book. Maybe you're just out of a relationship, and you're trying to determine your next steps. Or perhaps you've been divorced for a few months, and the idea of dating scares you beyond measure. Or finally, maybe you've exited a toxic relationship and want to figure out how NOT to date the same person with a different face.

Most of us coming out of relationships feel like some element of it was toxic. My last seven years have been spent educating men and women about narcissists. If you were in a relationship with a narcissist, my heart goes out to you. Even if a partner is not labeled or diagnosed with narcissism, relationships can be abusive and damaging.

When a Toxic Relationship Ends, the Pain Can be Worse

If you were in a toxic relationship, you'll need to give yourself longer to recover. You need to break the trauma bonds, which are unhealthy bonds we develop with an abuser. Secondly, the toxic person likely painted a picture of a great life the two of you would have together. This is called future faking. Then, when you least expected it, it was gone. Poof. Like your plans never existed.

Trauma bonds - We become addicted to the highs of the relationship, like heroin, and we suffer the lows, like withdrawal, just to reach the high again. We must stop that cycle. Therapy and coaching can significantly help with that. We will go through the steps of healing that worked for me in the next chapter.

Only You Label the End of a Relationship

Another thought I want to share with you is that people generally label "divorce" as being "negative." And yes, while there are ugly, painful downsides, there can also be a lot of positives that come out of a breakup or divorce. For example, I am the best version of myself that I have ever been post-divorce, and I hear the same from many divorce survivors. You get to know yourself again: your likes, your dislikes, and your passions. You can redefine yourself in a way that makes you happy. Ready to learn boating? You can. Are you ready to learn to hunt, fish, ride horses, take up fencing, country dance, waltz, or anything else? You can. No one is putting you in a box and labeling you without your permission. Take a risk and try something new.

"Where's my closure?!"

A woman called me the other day, sobbing. I could barely understand what Kirsten was saying because she was in so much pain. Her boyfriend had said nothing to her other than it was time to part ways, and Kirsten felt like she didn't have closure. Her heart was broken into a million pieces, and she felt like she couldn't go on. She kept crying that she just wanted to know why he'd left.

Closure means finding complete acceptance of what's happened so we can let go and move on. When we don't find closure, our hearts and minds can be held hostage waiting for an answer that will likely never come. We suffer, we don't understand, we miss the other person, and sometimes we call and beg to hear the reason why. But is the reason why ever enough?

Closure, especially after a toxic relationship, is a personal thing. We must take responsibility and find the closure ourselves so we can move on to better and greater things. Most of the time, we will not get it from the other person. In a few months or years, the reason may be clear, but we won't find it from anyone else.

Hindsight is 20/20, but until we get there, here are some ways to move on.

1. Disrespect is your closure.

If you were in a toxic relationship, their actions throughout your time together are closure. Think about the way they treated you. Maybe it was passive aggressive comments about your appearance. Maybe this ex was critical of your kids or family, or maybe this person told you that you were just too sensitive and too much to deal with.

How about this? Let's reframe it. Maybe they weren't enough for YOU.

People afraid of confrontation or unwilling to accept and discuss their part in the failure of a relationship aren't worth your time. Do you really want to be with someone like that? A healthy relationship encompasses two people doing their parts both separately and as a couple.

2. Ask yourself these tough questions.

A. Does holding on make you happy? I know the answer to this, but sometimes we need to ask ourselves that question.

B. Is there any reason that would be enough? That conversation with an ex would be like falling down a rabbit hole. I've been guilty of this. Years ago, I tried to have a conversation with an ex about why, and he gave me a lame reason. So, I begged for him to take me back. When he said "No," I cried harder, and I left his apartment a slobbering mess. Embarrassing, right?

C. What are you trying to avoid by holding on? Is it because grieving hurts? Is this ending a loss that reminds you of something else?

3. Grieve.

Let it out. Cry, scream, talk to friends, or watch sad movies. At this point, you need to release your emotions. They need to come out. If we don't grieve, the emotions can come out in unhealthy ways, like eating too much or too little, drinking too much alcohol, taking drugs, yelling at our kids, missing work, and more.

I was talking to a teenage girl the other day, and she said, "Miss Laura, sometimes I just need a Friday night under my covers watching Netflix after a long week at school." You know what I call that? Self-care. It's okay to lick our wounds, rest, and recharge for the future.

4. Use a ritual.

After some of the most difficult breakups I've had, I have burned the mementos from that person. Cards, letters, and dried flowers have all gone into the fireplace. Once, I even burned some in the driveway, leaving a black mark that can be seen on bright, sunny days. I have also sent a boyfriend's T-shirts and other gifts to charity. Having a process of letting go can speed up the acceptance of the change in your mind and heart. Notice I didn't call the breakup a loss. Why? Because every single time, looking back, a breakup is a good thing. Had I ended up with these men I once cried over, I would have lost me.

5. Block them and stop stalking their social media.

If I could arrest some of my friends for stalking their ex's social media accounts, I would. Nothing ever good comes of it. Nothing. All that creeping around on social media never helps, it only hurts.

"But Laura," some men and women have told me. "I just want to see how they're doing. I love them."

My answer is no, you don't want to see how they're doing. For example, let's say you see your ex with someone else. There's pain and tears. Then you go down another rabbit hole of asking yourself, "Will this person be happier with them?" (NO.) Also, you may ask, "What about me wasn't good enough?" (It's not you.)

More drastically, perhaps your ex had a parent pass away. The question might be, "Why didn't they call me? Don't I mean enough to them?" Then you fall face first down yet another rabbit hole, this one of extremism. And it is difficult to climb out of that without months of professional help.

I hope you understand where I am coming from. Block your ex across the board if you must. You can be "friends" later if you feel like it, but right now, it's about you and your healing. Let someone else deal with their crap.

Block them on your phone and email too, unless you have kids together. Then just use email or a court-approved app. No texts or calls. Studies show that a person's voice, picture, or even handwriting can trigger you and make you replay the movie in your head about when times were good. Remember, that was a film in your head. Movies aren't real. If what you had was authentic for both of you, it would've lasted. I know that hurts, but it is even more reason to move on and not look back.

Richard Paul Evans once said, *"It has been a mistake living my life in the past. One cannot ride a horse backwards and still hold its reins."*

Philosopher Soren Kierkegaard said, *"Life can be only understood backwards but it must be lived forwards."*

My favorite quote comes from Dr. Henry Cloud in his book *Necessary Endings*. Cloud wrote, *"I've seen too many circumstances where not executing an ending caused more pain than it solved."*

If you leave a wrecked relationship in your lane, you can't move forward and live your best life. Clear your path, and let's move on. You deserve it.

When Do I Date Again?

Date when you feel like you have done most of your healing work. Healing isn't linear and continues throughout life, but there is a point where you tell yourself, "I think I am okay. This isn't so bad, and I am excited about the future." That is the best time to start dating. Hurt people hurt people. Healthy people attract healthy people.

I will digress here for a second. Let me explain the phrase "hurt people hurt people" when it comes to dating since I have firsthand experience.

I dated a man I'll call Ethan. Ethan was funny, smart, and successful. We enjoyed going to the lake, watching movies, riding horses, and experiencing unfamiliar places around the world together. However, Ethan had unhealed trauma from childhood that would be detrimental to any relationship, even a friendship. There was sexual and physical abuse in his childhood, for which he had not had therapy.

This combination made intimacy, both emotional and physical, challenging for him. Ethan craved closeness, but he had a history of people closest to him not protecting him, abandoning him, and physically injuring him. Ethan had not experienced a safe place in this world. Any relationship with him would end in abandonment because he was playing out what he had learned over and over in childhood. No matter how great his needs had been as a little boy, people had left. People had hurt him, leaving this child to conquer his own demons and heal. No child knows how to do that.

Like some adults, Ethan didn't want therapy for something that had happened forty years ago. Whenever we would return home after a trip or spending a few days together, he would disappear. It hurt him too much to get close. For a woman who yearns for closeness and intimacy—like myself—every time he pulled away, it hurt me deeply. Eventually the days or weeks apart put too much strain on the relationship, and we broke up.

That, my friends, is how hurt people hurt people.

Keep An Open Mind

Be open to changing how you view the world. When you move on from a toxic relationship, you will lose people you thought were your friends. Many will be jealous because you had the strength to leave. Your actions will make them look in the mirror and acknowledge their own weaknesses, and that's a painful image to see. Yet, you'll gain others as friends that you never knew would get your back. It's refreshing, and a great way to start over. Embrace what an adventure life can be!

Briefly, here is what I am going to help you do during our healing work in Chapter 3.

1. **Allow yourself to grieve**. The emotions you're feeling want and need to surface, so permit yourself to let them out. If necessary, schedule a time for grieving. Work and home life can get in the way, and you don't want to unintentionally erupt when it could hurt your job performance or children. Foregoing the grieving process can set up roadblocks and guarantee disaster for future relationships.

    The five stages of grief you will go through are denial, anger, bargaining, depression, and acceptance. These are a part of the framework that makes up our learning to live without the person we once loved.

    Divorce is an emotional minefield for most people going through it. For example, someone may find themselves relieved and smiling one day, then distraught and crying the next. The complexity of feelings to process can be overwhelming, but there are ways to survive and set yourself up for your best life yet. However, grieving isn't linear, so you may move from one stage to the next, then regress two steps. There is no roadmap or correct way to grieve. There's an adage that says grieving is personal. And it is. Everyone grieves differently. The point is to let your grief out. Foregoing the grieving process can set up roadblocks and guarantee disaster for future relationships.

2. **Give yourself grace**. One of the most challenging things to do after a divorce or breakup is to forgive yourself. You are not a failure.

    In 2021, the divorce rate fell by 11 percent on average in the United States. However, the number of marriages taking place also decreased significantly. Understand that you are not alone. Sometimes when a relationship disintegrates, the downfall can be attributed more to one partner than the other. But, many times, the relationship just didn't work. These are two people that don't need to experience life together for the rest of their lives. Marriages can have expiration dates. One or both partners may mature or change, and expectations evolve with that. Don't chastise yourself. Learn what you can from the divorce and move on.

3. **Heal**. Healing is the most critical step during and after a divorce. The person who hurt you isn't coming back to fix things. You must take responsibility for your healing.

   There are many ways to heal, and there is no right way. Options for healing include but aren't limited to therapy, life coaching, spiritual healing, divorce classes, books, videos, and more. Those who heal the quickest use a combination of modalities that they find helpful. You get out of healing what you invest in it.

4. **Don't isolate.** It's easy to sit at home and watch sad movies, eat ice cream, and mourn what was. Sure, that's okay for a time. But the more you isolate, the more you stay in your head and open yourself up to alcohol or drug abuse to "just get through tonight."

   Instead, make yourself get out and see friends or invite them over. Integrate yourself into society once again. You will need to be careful not to overdo socializing. Sometimes being around many people can soothe your soul, but you aren't processing what you need to process. Find the best scenario for you.

5. **Wait to date**. Some therapists tell clients not to date for a year or more. However, you know yourself best. If isolation makes you depressed and suicidal, get out there when you feel strong enough. Dating doesn't mean you jump headfirst into a relationship. You'll need to do some healing first. Many people carry their problems with them, and when two hurting people get together, that's a recipe for disaster.

   Those who seem to have the healthiest relationships after a divorce are those who waited until they felt "ready," stronger, and healed. Hurt people hurt people, especially when dating too quickly after a divorce.

You can find Laura's video on these five tips on her YouTube channel here: https://youtu.be/Kh1RBJH7nmI

CHAPTER 4

COPING WITH REJECTION AND LONELINESS

I don't want anyone who doesn't want me – Oprah Winfrey

Rejection

Few things in life hurt more than rejection. Whether we are rejected for a job, a promotion, or by a person we love, rejection hurts. I've witnessed friends survive job loss, major career setbacks, and the loss of a home, but I've never seen people hurt more than they do from a heartbreak stemming from rejection. I thought this topic deserves its own chapter because rejection has been and will always be a part of dating. You will reject some people who want your love, and some potential partners we adore will spurn us. It's how we deal with the denial that determines our future.

It's how we deal with the denial that determines our future.

My worst story of rejection happened right after my divorce. I had met Doug in 2015, and we'd dated a few times, then gone our separate ways. In October of 2016, we revisited our connection despite my counselor's direction on avoiding relationships so soon after divorce. Anyway, I dove right into one with Doug. Unsurprisingly, this man was another narcissist, if not a sociopath. Since I had done little healing work, I attracted the bad boys or narcissists and was intensely attracted to Doug. Anyway, I thought I loved this man and wanted to marry him. We dated eight months.

It was a swift courtship with a tumultuous ending. We went from talking about houses with enough room for all the kids in October to Doug flying to Germany for two weeks in May without saying goodbye. And wow, was that breakup painful. Doug had disappeared, while at the same time my ex-husband was calling me terrible names, my cocker spaniel was getting sick, and I had the flu. I lost ten pounds in two weeks because all I could do was cry.

By August, I came out of my sorrow and started to live life again. I vowed to myself that I would never get hurt this badly again.

The Science Behind the Pain of Rejection

Cocaine increases the amount of the feel-good hormone dopamine in the brain, and not surprisingly, so does romantic love. That's one reason breakups feel like undergoing the agony of drug-withdrawal symptoms when you are apart from the person you deeply love. If you don't love or have feelings for someone, you likely won't experience the agony of a breakup. Most people in their lifetime will deal with a broken heart.

Drug withdrawal is a physiological response to the sudden quitting or slowing of use of a substance to which the body has grown dependent on.[6] Most people struggle when withdrawing from opioids, such as heroin and cocaine, two of the medications that give the best "rush" and sense of euphoria. Withdrawal symptoms can be different combinations of physi-cal, mental, and emotional factors—some of which can prove dangerous if left unmanaged. Breakups can be the same way. You are going to need emotional and physical support to get through a breakup or recover from a toxic relationship.

Researchers are understanding more about heartbreak and how brain activity resembles an addict coming off an additive substance. Dr. Karen Fisher, an anthropologist and researcher at the Kinsey Institute at Indi-ana University, decided to investigate one of the most powerful sensations anyone can feel: romantic love. Fisher conducted MRIs (scans of the brain) on thirty-seven people who had just been dumped. She found regions in five areas of the brain that are active after a breakup. These regions are linked to the following:

1. Intense romantic love

2. Deep attachment

3. Cravings and addictions

4. Physical pain

5. Figuring out gains and losses[7]

Fisher discovered several consistencies in her research. People suffer-ing from a breakup often had a reward system in overdrive, because when we can't get what we want, we crave it more. Fisher's research also revealed that many "dumpees" presented with three traits found with addiction: toler-ance, withdrawals, and relapse. She described the symptoms of addiction in these subjects as obsession, losing sense of self, intense cravings, a tendency to distort reality, and profound sadness and need.

Plato said it best when the philosopher wrote, *The god of love lives in a state of need. It is a need. It is an urge. It is a homeostatic imbalance. Like hunger and thirst, it's almost impossible to stamp out.*[8]

Getting Past Rejection, Even When Your Ex is Toxic

There is a caveat when it comes to moving past rejection. If you have been in a relationship with a narcissist or other toxic person, it will take longer to heal. There are a few reasons for that.

Your reality wasn't your reality. It belonged to your ex.

If we are in a toxic relationship, the toxic partner often defines almost everything about us. They are skilled at delivering subtle insinuations or downright commands about how we manage our appearance, beliefs, values, morals, money, work, and children. We begin to doubt ourselves in every aspect of life, so we turn to the toxic person, who seems to know it all. Our confidence disappears, and it takes time to get this back.

Their voices stay in our heads.

Have you ever heard a jingle from a commercial that won't stop playing in your head? You walk through the day, and you think, "I don't want to sing this tune about laundry detergent anymore!" That's what happens after dating or marrying a narcissist or toxic person. We can continue to hear their words for weeks, months, and years, until we do the healing work that's needed. It's only then that the phrases that destroyed us become whispers, and then, there's blessed silence.

When I left a toxic ex, he told me, "You can't compete with the other women in Dallas. Good luck finding someone who will love you like I love you."

The first few years after my divorce, I was too shy to walk into Starbucks because I thought people would laugh at me due to my irrelevance and brokenness. My ex had told me that everyone thought I was crazy, too skinny, and a dumb blonde. I literally would drive a few extra miles to find a coffee shop with a drive through.

It's possible to get past these voices by putting in time to heal and process how ridiculous the toxic person can be. I now walk in Starbucks or any other coffee shop wearing workout clothes and zero make up. Who cares? Other people are too busy with their own problems to worry about me.

They poison others against you.

Maybe you live in a small community, suburb, or apartment building. Don't expect the toxic ex to say anything complimentary about you. This person will likely want to destroy your reputation.

Here's the catch with these antics. If people really know you and how special you are, they won't believe a word your ex says. If they do believe the lies, then you don't want someone with so little substance and character as a friend anyway.

There is a way past rejection. Let's couple the science behind the pain with concrete steps toward healing.

Go No Contact

First, we need to go no contact. This includes no communication, no stalking their social media, and no drive by late at night to see if the ex is home. There are healthier ways to fill that void left in the person's wake. For example, drug addicts cannot wean themselves off the drug to which they are addicted. They must have another substance, like Methadone or Suboxone, to temper their cravings as they get better. The addict cannot approach the drug of addiction and have just a taste. It's typically all or nothing for the addict, and this goes during the withdrawal phase of relationships, too. Replace the nothing with something healthier. You can't even have a taste of this person or the life they are living without you.

For me, after a breakup or any setback, I try to make something good come out of the pain. After being rejected by Doug, I found my first life coach. I was scrolling through Twitter and came across a conference that Rebecca Lynn Pope had held as part of T. D. Jakes's "Megafest" in 2017. It was a twenty-second clip, but her strength, gutsy attitude, and kind demeanor stood out to me. I was at the lowest I had ever been, and I was ready to try anything. I scheduled a session with her and never looked back.

Out of my work with Rebecca came my first Amazon #1 Best Seller *Ugly Love*. Writing has always been part of my therapy, first through a journalism career and now as an author. I wrote for months about the pain of my childhood, divorce, being a single mom, and breakup.

I am not sure what your passion is, but channel it toward something good. When you turn that negative energy into something positive, it really is kind of like a "f@#$ you" to your ex. And it feels so good!

Reframe the Rejection

Secondly, this is probably the biggest point I want to make in the entire book: rejection is a blessing in disguise. There's a reason for the rejection, and although you don't see it today, you will see it later, and you will be relieved. You will say to yourself, "Thank the LAWD that didn't work out," or "I dodged a bullet back then!"

Rejection is a blessing in disguise.

I have taken many classes by Transformational Leader Dr. Dharius Daniels, and some of the phrases I have learned from him and others in my class are below. These words can soothe a broken heart and soul.

- **Rejection is your protection** – We can't see the future, but whether you believe in karma, the universe, God, or another higher power, your higher power can see what's ahead. This rejection happened to protect you. What if this guy you loved was a serial cheater and you never saw it? What if this woman was going to decide mid-marriage that she didn't want children, and you've always dreamed of having a family? What if this person has a gambling addiction, and you just dodged having your entire life savings disappear? Hug yourself. Take a deep breath. You are okay and will be better than ever.

- **Rejection is new direction** – Sometimes, rejection is also pointing us to where our destination ultimately is. Would I have authored a best-selling book and helped thousands of people without Doug dumping me? No. I was spending all my time doting on him! I barely had time to write my boss an email, much less write an entire manuscript. Look at the direction that you're headed now due to the breakup. If you don't know where you're headed, that's okay, too. Sit on it. It will surface when you least expect it.

- **If they can't accept your past, then they don't deserve to be in your future** – This phrase stands alone. If you are trying to build a future with someone, and they've rejected you because of your past, good. Why would you want to be with someone who doesn't accept everything about you? Your past has made you the amazing person that you are! You may be more empathetic and sincere due to your past. You survived your past, so celebrate it! If this person can't do that with you, then it's their loss.

- **Don't go back if the reason you left is still there** – So often, we (me!) give people second, third, and fourth chances. We go back after hearing the right words or apologies, yet when we find ourselves in the middle of the relationship again, nothing has changed. Nothing. Therefore, *we must watch someone's actions over their words*. It's easy to make promises, but do they stick? Has this person sought self-improvement and healing through therapy, coaching, or support groups? There's your answer on giving it another go. My guess is the answer is no. Most people don't think relationship issues are their fault, and they don't want to do the work to change if they are indeed the problem. If someone goes to counseling and works on their side of things, you have a keeper. Stick around and see where this relationship goes. Watch for consistency and sincerity.

- **Stop the regret** - Regret won't undo the relationship. Stop dissecting the past. Quit thinking about every aspect of the relationship that went south. We all make mistakes. If it was your mistake that led to the breakup, then acknowledge it and let it go. Learn a lesson from it and keep putting one foot in front of the other. If you live in the past, you will never find what's best for you in the future. If it was the plan of God or the Universe for this relationship to work, it would have. Don't mourn but celebrate! Your dream life is just around the corner. Don't miss it by looking back.

Here are some other tips to help you move past rejection:

1. **Don't badmouth the other person.** You know what this person is like behind closed doors and that's all that matters. The farther away you get from the relationship, the clearer your vision will be. Don't try to convince anyone how bad your ex is. Don't try to teach the ex how bad they are, either. Walk away with your head held high. It's their loss.

2. **Don't rule out friendship, at some point.** Do not try to be friends now. Now is the time for no contact so you can fill that emptiness with healthier things. Being friends now would be too confusing for your heart and mind.

3. **Don't beg them to change their mind.** I have done this, too. Don't be embarrassed. But now that you know how unhealthy it is, and how you lose part of your dignity, don't beg someone to stay. Begging won't make it better. Your ex won't see a lightbulb go off and think, "I must have this person back! Right now!" Keep your dignity. It feels so good later and helps you get stronger faster.

4. **Understand rejection is a normal part of life.** Rejection happens in many parts of our lives. From children who reject a rule that we set to our bodies rejecting a tainted food, rejection happens. Accept it, learn from it, grieve it, and move on.

5. **Recognize the feelings it brings up and get help if you need to.** I had to get help when I moved two thousand miles away to work in a small town as a television reporter and anchor. The

community was full of transplants, and it was difficult to meet friends. I was lonely, sad, and slept a lot. Once I realized I was depressed, I got help. My doctor put me on Prozac, and I began seeing a therapist. Within a few weeks I was on the mend. I could see the good in my situation, no matter how dire it had seemed at first.

6. **Think about the future.** Start thinking about what you could be doing a year from now. A lot can change in a year or even a day! You can get a new job, buy a home, meet a new best friend, fall in love, or win some money. The future is yours if you put yourself out there and live life.

7. **Journal about the relationship**. Write in a journal about the relationship. I tell my clients that have been through narcissistic abuse to make a list of all their ex's bad traits—and I mean all of them. If your ex used to sneeze messily and loudly, write that down. If their drinking became a huge thorn in your relationship, or their kids were brats, document that, too. This keeps you from going back when they are begging you to come back, because most likely they will. Review that list, count your blessings, and move on.

8. **Time heals**. I know, I hate this phrase, too. But you will heal, and you will find love and happiness again. Do the right things, and that will happen more quickly than you can imagine.

Coping with Loneliness

"The most terrible poverty is loneliness and the feeling of being unloved."
—Mother Teresa

DATING STORY #5

Mr. Fill the Void

I had been texting with a man I met on Bumble for several days. Physically he was tall, had salt-and-pepper hair, and a great smile. Emotionally and intellectually, he could communicate succinctly yet eloquently. We met for a drink after about a week of messaging, and during our conversation, he told me he was fifty-two and had just ended an eight-month relationship a few days before. For me, that seemed a little premature to be out dating again. He was clearly hurting.

As an empath, I can feel others' emotions. Waves of sadness and pain emanated from Paul. I knew no matter how good our date was, things between us wouldn't work. He had so much pain from his previous relationship, all he was thinking about was her. I was merely a distraction. He had a void he needed to fill. The date ended, and even though we texted a few times, I let the conversations fade to black. I'd learned my lesson early on about trying to help someone heal more quickly so we could date. Paul needed to heal in his own way, by himself, before he could offer another person what they deserved.

Paul likely compared his next seven or more dates to his previous girlfriend. His sadness and ambivalence may have even hurt other women who took his actions personally. Before dating, everyone needs to heal from previous hurts. There's nothing more important. It's not plug and play. You can't stick someone new in the vacancy and have the hurt disappear.

We All Want to Matter

We all want to feel loved and important. Some of our greatest fears may be growing old without anyone to care for or without anyone caring for us.

Being single can often feel lonely. We might feel like we will never find our person or we aren't worthy of love. It's easy to feel sorry for ourselves and believe that this moment in time mirrors what our lives will always be. This isn't true. We are lying to ourselves. This is one day, not a predictor of our entire future.

What Loneliness Is

An article in Psychology Today written by Arash Emanzadeh, a researcher in neuropsychology and general psychology, breaks down loneliness as a feeling with two parts. Loneliness is an unpleasant experience in which one perceives a relationship deficit, whether it's in the quality or quantity of one's relationships. It leaves the lonely person often feeling anxious, unsatisfied, and depressed. [9]

As we will discover in the coming paragraphs, it depends on the person's predilections as to how and why they feel lonely. Personally, I feel lonely when I don't have an emotional connection with a friend or partner. Yet, I've met men and women who dismiss an emotional tie with a partner but require a physical bond. And finally, some others must date someone who draws attention to their relationship, so they become the couple everyone surrounds and envies.

Reasons People are Lonely

While **heredity** is the number one factor, there are other reasons a person might feel lonely.[10]

- **Environment**

- **Circumstances**

- **Thoughts and attitudes**

- History of abuse

- Hostile/intrusive or withdrawn/inattentive parents

- Disorganized or anxious ambivalent attachment style and problems with communication

- Internalization of parent/attachment figures

- Feelings of hostility or helplessness

It's important to look at why you are feeling alone. For me, a history of abuse comes into play. I must be careful not to fill my head with negative thoughts and voices from toxic people in my past. Again, I remind myself that being lonely today doesn't mean I will be lonely tomorrow.

What works for me is to write. Writing is therapeutic. If I hadn't been lonely periodically, I would not have finished this manuscript. There are other suggestions below, but primarily, find something you love. Not a person, but a thing you adore doing. And do it! The next thing you'll know, the hours have passed and it's time to work or go have fun again.

Are Men Lonelier Than Women?

The trouble is that loneliness can lead us to make poor choices when to comes to dating. As humans, most of us are geared toward companionship. We want to do life with someone. That's why it saddened me when I came across research published in Psychology Today about the rise of single, lonely men.[11]

The research was done by a psychologist named Dr. Greg Matos, who specializes in relationships and family counseling. Matos made three key points:

- Dating opportunities for heterosexual men are diminishing as relationship standards rise.

- Men represent approximately 62 percent of dating app users, lowering their chances for matches.

- Men need to address skills deficits to meet healthier relationship expectations.

If we look at the first point about relationship standards, more women want to date men who work on themselves, whether it's through therapy or another avenue. Women often do this because we are typically more emotional than men.

Also, more women, according to Matos, want men with whom they can have an emotional connection, effective communication, and share values. Some men may have put up emotional walls due to past relationships or childhood pain, therefore hurting their abilities to have a connection and communicate about trivial and principal issues. This is where therapy can help.

Secondly, men may be the larger population on dating apps, but from what I've learned, some men may not be choosing wisely when it comes to long-term relationship potential. For example, my experiences in the dating world have shown me that often there are two buckets of men. The first bucket comprises those looking for a long-term relationship. They want to find their forever person. Then, there's another bucket, consisting of the men who want to play. I believe these men are the ones coming out of long marriages and bad relationships, or they are just men who want to have sex with as many women as possible before they start a family.

Anecdotally, it's not uncommon in Dallas and other large cities to see a newly divorced man dating a woman twenty-five years younger. It's about arm candy, ego, and money. The man gets the beautiful woman, and the woman gets access to his bank. Sure, there are some women who have it all: beauty, brains, and the bank. These women have their choice of men, and often, if they are serious about starting a family or partnering with someone, they choose someone closer to their generation.

I think after a few months or years of playing, some men try to find more. They want a woman who has had the same life experiences as they have, such as raising kids or getting second degrees. But when a man has established himself as a "player" who can bring home a supermodel, it's difficult to date someone from a different (older) generation. Some men won't feel happy with little emotional connection with their girl. For others, that doesn't matter. It's their partner's job to look gorgeous and be on their arm.

This is where the choice comes in that can lead a man to being lonely or fulfilled when they are in a rocking chair at ninety. Does a man want to be lonely and emotionally starved or check their ego at the door and find a woman to grow old with? It's a difficult choice for some men, and hopefully Matos's findings will give men something to think about.

Some women struggle with this, too. I dated a beautiful man. He was Greek, funny, and very skilled in bed. It was fun to walk into a restaurant and have people say, "You guys are a beautiful couple." Some of my friends asked me, "Damn girl. How did you pull that off?"

My insecurities about our relationship grew the more I fell for Mr. Greek God/Mr. Gorgeous. Could we bond over things that mattered to me, like raising kids? No, he didn't have or want any. Did he talk about God's purpose for his life? No, all Mr. Gorgeous focused on was money, crypto, and the gym. I know that's not all bad, and Mr. G was a good guy! But, when I was honest with myself, for the long term, he wasn't for me. I needed more of an emotional connection. I needed someone who liked to stay up late, talking about life, kids, retirement, love, aging parents, and more. (Sure, we can kiss and do more in between conversations, but I am a woman who needs both an emotional and physical connection.) Had Mr. Gorgeous and I stayed together, I would've been lonely. For me, it's better to be by myself than in a relationship where I feel alone. One day we all will be in rocking chairs, if we are lucky to live that long. I want to have a conversation with my soulmate while I am rocking in mine.

One of my good friends, Dan Rawls, divorced the same year I did, and his dating experiences have mirrored that of many men. Rawls said when he meets a woman, he can tell within the first twenty seconds whether she will go out with him again or pass on a second date. Why are we, as women, so judgmental? Not all women do this, but I found myself early on being picky about shallow things like looks, height, hair color, and more. Your prince charming or princess may be the opposite of what you imagined you would fall in love with. Get to know the person before you make a hasty decision. Be neutral until they show you who they are and what they stand for. If you genuinely want long-term, unconditional love, it may not come in the package to which you've been limiting yourself. I am not saying to date someone from a zombie apocalypse, but let's all scratch the surface before we kick someone to the curb for grey hair or a few extra pounds.

Looks fade but character doesn't.

What Do You Do When You're Lonely?

It's easy to dig a hole and crawl in it when we are lonely. We think the feeling of being alone and without a partner will last forever. I have great news: It won't. You will find your person, but you won't find them if you stay in your self-imposed exile too long.

Here are some ways to feel less lonely.

1. **Acknowledge your loneliness.** It's okay to be lonely. There are millions of people in marriages or crowded rooms that feel lonely. Heck, I chaperoned twenty teenagers to a country concert recently, and among the crazy kids and drunk college students, I felt completely alone.

    This one night or one season of your life doesn't determine your character or your future. It will be okay.

2. **Call a friend**. Pick up the phone and have a conversation with a buddy. You can talk about the weather or the shoes you just bought. Just connect with someone.

    If you are close to them, tell them you are feeling lonely. Ask them if they want to meet for a quick bite or drink. Break your monotony and get out.

3. **Get outside.** Sometimes all it takes is a breath of fresh air or seeing a lake or ocean to remind you that the world is huge. You are not alone. Remember, there are likely millions of other people feeling lonely at the same time. The world has around seven billion people in it. You are not by yourself suffering these feelings.

4. **Meet with a counselor or other mental health professional.** Many counselors have emergency lines for communication when a patient hits a big roadblock. Call them! If you are crying, feeling worthless, and can't get out of bed, please call them. You are too important to the world to leave it.

I've been there. There have been times I was so low that I gave the four Xanax pills I had for anxiety to my best friend. I knew that those may not kill me, but it was tempting to take all four and hope the pain and loneliness of the season I was in would leave. But don't do it. This day will pass, and tomorrow will be better. And the next day and the next day. Hang on and get help. Tell someone how much you are hurting. Sometimes we hit rock bottom before the world turns and life is good again.

If you feel like you might be a danger to yourself, you can text the National Suicide Hotline at 988.

CHAPTER 5

HEALING FROM THE PAST TO BE READY FOR LOVE

Many of us have had the unpleasant experience of a bad breakup, then eventually dating someone else who is the ex in a different body. This happens when we rush from one relationship to another.

This chapter give you a roadmap to healing. I charge thousands of dollars to my high-end clients for this information. These are people who are ready to finally put the past behind them and move on to an amazing life and true love. Don't discount this healing process. It can jumpstart your dating process and take you to another level when meeting or matching with potential partners.

DATING STORY #6

Mr. Repeat

I certainly know about dating too soon because I did that after my divorce. It had been just a few months since signing the legal papers, and I was still randomly bursting into tears in public places and forgetting to pay the electricity bill. Yes, I forgot there were bills that went along with my responsibilities as a single mom. I was glad to get my son fed and out the door for school and subsequently summer camp. Therefore, my power was turned off in the middle of a Texas summer. If I couldn't click and pay online, what in the world was I doing trying to find a new partner? I was hurting, that's what. I thought another boyfriend could relieve the pain.

Quickly, I met a guy who was my ex with a different face. I introduced you to Doug in Chapter Four. Doug told me everything I needed to hear: We were members of the same church, believed in family first, and worked hard in our careers. He had many bad similarities with the ex, too, from his controlling nature to his critical comments and passive aggressiveness. Yet, I loved him because it was what I was comfortable with.

Several months later, this guy ripped the rug out from under me. One week Doug was telling me that I was a part of his family. We could lead a Bible study and help other marriages grow stronger as we grew our own. We introduced our kids to each other's, and Doug even pointed out homes that would hold them all. Then suddenly, with no warning, Doug wouldn't return calls or texts. He was done with me. He told me this by ghosting me, which was exactly what my ex would have done. Doug hurt me deeply, and he hurt my son with his sudden change of heart.

Dating After Abuse

Dating after any type of abuse is difficult. When we are dating, we are vulnerable. In fact, I think dating can feel like a beauty pageant or a courtroom drama. You are putting yourself on a platform in front of judges, waiting for someone to measure your value when they don't know you. They are also assessing your beauty, intelligence, morals, integrity, and compassion.

Beauty pageants are based on judging the contestants' physical beauty, with an occasional question-and-answer session thrown in. Do the judges get to know these girls? Not really. Many people consider pageants to be misogynistic and racist because until recently, mostly white women made up the top ten contestants. Pageants also put an unhealthy emphasis on body size, although pageant directors might argue the trend has moved from skinny to "healthy." However, when's the last time you saw an obese woman win a pageant? Some trauma survivors, like myself, developed eating disorders to cope with our lack of control and pain. We couldn't stand being judged, so we needed to control what we could in the face of someone deciding our fate. For abusers, we were never good enough, no matter how many times we were judged.

Dating feels like a pageant and more so because we have no control over what people think about us. We are powerless over the lens through which another person looks at us. Your date could be having a difficult day, could be attracted to only tall brunettes, or be sick. Yet their attraction or lack thereof can hurt us if we take it personally, and many trauma survivors do. Our parents or other adults told us in our childhood that when anything went wrong, it was our fault, so we believe that when dating doesn't go well, it all comes down to us.

Here's a secret: It's not about you. I promise.

Here's a secret: It's not about you. It's not. I promise. There is someone or several people for everyone on this earth. You won't be everyone's flavor of ice cream, and they won't be yours. Some men like blondes, while others prefer to date redheads. Some like tiny, while the guy down the street likes voluptuous. Some women like tall men, while others put fitness at the top of their lists no matter the height. Some men like short hair while others are attracted to long hair. And finally, understand that some people, like me, are attracted to intelligence, kindness, and Godliness over anything and everything else.

More Baggage than DFW Airport

The older we grow, the more pain we have. When I was in television news at a station in Dallas, I worked with a reporter named John Pronk. In the newsroom we called him Pronkster. Pronkster was a great man and storyteller, so much so he won awards for his television work profiling influential Texans. One day, as he regaled us with stories about his children, he mentioned that he had been married four times. Of course, as a young, inquisitive reporter with absolutely no filter, I asked him why.

Pronkster said, "I am just not good at it, Laura. I have more baggage than the number four carousel at DFW International Airport."

I remember laughing so hard I began crying. But John was right! Marriage after marriage or relationship after relationship without healing just adds pain on top of pain. It adds baggage on top of baggage. Eventually no one can carry the weight of that. Heck, a SmartCart won't even work.

The burden grows heavier when you add the other person in the relationship who also hasn't done the work. Combined, you have two people who may likely damage each other even more. That's why I told you the stories about Paul and John. When we aren't healed, a new relationship is a bandage to a wound in which blood seeps through. It just won't work.

Hurt People Attract Hurt People. Healed People Attract Healed People.

The dating app Hinge recently did a survey of singles who are dating. Ninety-one percent said they would prefer to date someone who is in therapy. Eighty nine percent said when a person mentions therapy on the first date, they are likely to want a second one.[12]

So, get to work.

How to Heal from Your Past and Jump-Start Your Future

I can give you my word on this: unless you do your healing work, you will not find the love of your life. You may find love and a relationship, but it won't be "your" person. You will be settling for average or inadequate. Hurt people not only hurt people, they also attract hurt people. And when two damaged souls end up together, you find two people trying to fix each other. You can also develop an unhealthy bond with that person as you compete to be the one who is the most broken. I've seen this with clients and people in my support group many times.

You may be asking yourself, "But wouldn't two broken people have a special bond?" Absolutely. But if you don't go to therapy and work on healing as individuals and as a couple, one partner can emerge like a butterfly from a cocoon, ready to spread its wings and see the world. Meanwhile, the other partner is left wondering what happened.

WHAT YOU NEED TO KNOW ABOUT THE HEALING WORK

Trauma

Trauma can strip even the strongest person of their self-esteem and self-worth. Many trauma survivors they felt like the shell of the person they once were. Even if you've been through little trauma, a breakup can cause stress and a diminished self-esteem.

As with any trauma or unhealthy relationship, you can call yourself a victim until you understand that you didn't ask for this. You didn't date or marry that person to be abused, and you certainly couldn't choose the parents to whom you were born. That's what being a victim means. You were likely innocently living life, maybe even enjoying it, and along came this toxic person who portrayed themselves as your soulmate and your everything.

Like many trauma survivors have told me, you weren't really attracted to this person. You thought, "Hey. They seem great and are fun to spend time with. I'll see where this goes."

Then off came the mask, and Jekyll morphed into Hyde. Yet, like so many of us often do, you stayed when this happened. When we find ourselves in a toxic relationship, we convince ourselves that the real person will reappear any minute now. The abuse and agony of the relationship continues, and we think when it stops, we will have a stronger bond than other couples we know. We tell ourselves that this relationship is special!

When we do exit a toxic relationship, it can be difficult to fully extricate ourselves. We leave avenues open for this person to reach out to us. We may still accept texts from them. Or, if we have blocked them on our phones, we leave an avenue open through social media, such as allowing them access through Facebook or Instagram to private message us.

When you understand you have zero responsibility for that person's actions, you become a survivor. There is nothing you did or didn't do to cause this.

When you leave, cut off all contact. I can almost promise you they will still find a way to communicate with you. That said, this is my most important advice of all time regarding toxic people: keep a card in your bag or wallet that says, "Sometimes the realization of what is going to happen helps to keep it from happening." Read it before you respond or give this person yet another chance. They DON'T CHANGE. If there was a discard and he immediately took up with someone else or many others, then he will do that again. The same goes for a woman who has been toxic. Stay away. The love of your life is around the corner. You can't find them when you are hooked on the past.

Triggers –If you're human, you have triggers. (Now that I think about it, dogs and other animals have triggers, too. Charlie, my chocolate-brown labradoodle, plants all fours on the concrete and won't move when we arrive at the vet's office. I must carry him in like a sack of heavy potatoes. Charlie fears the animal clinic because the doctor often takes a fecal sample, during which he cries like a screech owl.) As humans, it's what we do with those triggers that matters. Perhaps you have a trigger that when a door slams, you imagine your ex-husband returning home from work, once again angry and ready to take it out on you. Do you cower or shake? Or do you gently remind yourself it's just your teenage daughter in a hurry to come inside from the rain?

For me, the silent treatment prompts me to revert to the mindset of a teenager. That's when I wanted to be heard the most and loved unconditionally. However, when I didn't perform to a toxic parent's standards, that parent would withhold attention and love. "I sacrifice so much for you, and now this," a toxic parent will often say.

Toxic partners or parents often use the silent treatment to tell someone that they aren't worthy enough to be spoken to or included in a conversation. The silent treatment can last minutes, hours, days, or months.

Such occurrences seldom happen in a stable environment, so if this was your childhood, you may not have many triggers. In a healthy family, the parents meet the needs of the children physically, emotionally, intellectually, and spiritually. However, in a toxic family, the roles are reversed. The child must validate the parent, whether through their actions or words. The kids must shine a light on mom or dad, because really, it's always about the toxic parent. The children can't develop their own beliefs, values, morals, ethics, and talents because the unhealthy parent dictates those. Most of the time, but not always, the dictator in the family is a narcissist.

When we grow up in a disruptive, unhealthy environment, we carry that damage with us into adulthood. That's why it's important to understand your triggers. That way you can take a minute, an hour, or an entire day and figure out your next steps.

HEALING PART 1

This section of the book may take you a few hours, days, or weeks to master. I want you to dive into your healing process. It's there you will improve your chances of finding true love. You'll discover that you react less to your triggers and make smarter choices about relationships. We cannot be ruled by our emotions and make good decisions. Working through your deepest feelings now will help you for the rest of your life.

Working through your deepest feelings now will help you the rest of your life.

If following these instructions in the book is too much, I have an e-course available on Thinkific if you prefer the video version. Each video walks you through a different step. The course also comes with a workbook. After you finish this version on Thinkific, you can skip to Chapter 3.

Order the course here: https://lauracharanza.thinkific.com/

The first thing I want you to do is give up social media for a month. I understand that if your job entails posting on platforms, then you don't have this choice. I am specifically referring to scrolling endlessly through others' Instagram and Facebook pages. This habit can be toxic. Comparison is the thief of joy and your healing process. There is a reason some call Instagram "Insta-sham" and Facebook "Fakebook." You are seeing the highlight reel of someone's life when the rest of it may be a horror movie.

The second thing I want you to do is set aside fifteen minutes a day to meditate and pray. If you aren't comfortable praying, then you can skip that part. What we're doing here is teaching our minds to slow down and focus. Mediation has been proven to help with stress since it can reduce cortisol levels, which contribute to the fight or flight syndrome.

You can just be still with your eyes closed, or you can do a guided mediation. I like the apps Headspace and Calm. I started meditating by sitting in the grass in my backyard, closing my eyes, and counting my breaths.

Do this for a week before moving on to part two. I want you to dig deep into yourself and what you want for the future.

HEALING PART TWO

Your Trauma Timeline

First, get out several sheets of paper or a posterboard. You are going to make a trauma timeline.

Remember when we were in elementary school, and we had to make a timeline of a war or Columbus sailing to America? That's what you will do here. You will start with your first painful memory and continue through today.

You can use arbitrary dates when you don't remember them exactly. It's more about placing the trauma on paper so you can see all that you've been through. Congratulate yourself as you do this. Some people truly have been through nothing. You have. You're still standing, and the best part of your life is yet to come.

Some examples: (December 9, 1974). My first traumatic memory is when my baby brother came home from the hospital. I was three, and I wanted to hold him. My mother told me, "No." I can see Mother holding him in a blanket while she sat on my grandmother's plaid sofa. I felt deeply hurt and no longer part of the family. Even though I couldn't verbalize it then, I feared he was becoming the most important part of the family equation. By the way, my brother is a great man and father to his own kids. Mom has always said he was the easy child. He didn't demand nurturing or display a strong will about making his own choices, while I did. As the firstborn and same sex child, I felt the most pressure to perform.

Another example: (September 2013). I interviewed for a new job at a company. This sales role meant more money and flexibility. The role involved selling a medication for a rare liver disease in children, and I wanted to help babies while being paid for it. It was my dream job. Before I left for the interview, I asked my husband why he wasn't saying good luck. Shane said, "Well, I don't want to build you up because when you fail, I must pick you up all over again." Ouch.

As my son would say, "I killed it." I got the job! Nevertheless, the trauma of my husband believing in my failure stuck with me and deeply hurt me.

Nothing is off-limits for the timeline. Put the incident down, no matter how silly or inconsequential it seems. We are looking for patterns in your life and the repetition of the people involved. Most importantly, you can witness first-hand what you've been through. Later, you will be astonished and proud of yourself.

You don't have to share this timeline with me or anyone else. This work is the first building block of your healing. You've got this.

HEALING PART 3

Healing Letters

This is the most crucial part of the healing process. Looking at your timeline, identify three people who have hurt you the most. You may even think of them without looking at your work, or you may pinpoint five or six people.

Find a notebook or several sheets of paper and a pen. We are going to do some writing the old-school way. You are going to write a letter to each of these three people who you feel damaged you. The perpetrator will never read it, and you don't have to share it with anyone else.

Allocate as much time as you need for the first letter, and find a quiet place to write it. I prefer to write my healing letters when no one is home and it's quiet. As you start to write, I want you to hold nothing back. Nothing. Whatever you have wanted to say to this person, say it as if you are standing in front of them and they cannot respond. Scream, cry, yell, whisper, or hit a pillow while you compose. Get those feelings out. Write until you are exhausted and have said all you can say. Put that letter away, and plan future time to write the second and third letters.

This is a process I complete every few years because we all have people that hurt us. Again, healing isn't linear. You may reach a point where you feel fantastic, but that doesn't mean you won't struggle with something or someone significant. This is a practice you can use repeatedly.

HEALING PART FOUR

Burning Your Letters

This is one of the easiest but most significant part of your healing journey. You can ask a friend or confidante to do this with you, or you can do this by yourself. If you want me to pray with you or talk you through the burning process, you can book a session here: https://charanzacoachingsession.as.me/

Gather your letters and find a fireplace, firepit, or any other safe place to burn these compositions. After you light a fire, sit still, and watch the flames for a minute. Understand that as you burn these letters, you are releasing the bad energy and pain people have left you with. The Universe (or God) will take this grief from you. It is no longer your heavy burden to carry. Let it go!

As a woman of faith, I pray before I burn the letters, then I pray as I throw each into the fire. Again, if you need to cry or sob or yell, I hope you'll do so. It's important for you to grieve fully to move on.

Once you've scorched the letters, sit silently, and reflect on the relief you will feel. The Universe has your pain and suffering now. You may need to do this often until the pain is completely released. I still write and burn such letters when I am going through a tough time in my life.

HEALING PART 5

Celebration Timeline

Now it's time to turn the corner! We are drawing a line in the sand. The pain is behind you, and your future is bright and waiting! We will not dwell in the past, although sometimes we will need to revisit issues and understand why we are triggered. Let it go so your lane or aisle is clear for the remarkable things and people ahead!

Take out a few more sheets of paper. We are making another time-line, and this time it is to be filled with good events or things in your life. Good things you might recall for your timeline include the birth of a child or grandchild, your first job, the day you met your first boyfriend, or the day you received a huge bonus at work. The list can go on.

For example, one of my fondest memories is of the day I met my best friend, Holly Houser. She was thirteen and I was twelve. We would go on vacations together with our families when we were preteens and teens. We giggled and pestered our little brothers until they ran crying to Mom. Holly was there when I told her about my first kiss and vice versa.

Don't get me wrong. We also stirred up trouble when we could. One evening, we decided we would sneak out with a twelve-pack of toilet paper and "roll" the trees of a home down the street. Two boys lived there, and we knew they would be angry to spend a Saturday picking toilet paper out of their trees.

In the dark of night, after sneaking out around 3 a.m., we covered those tall oaks with rolls of paper so thick you couldn't see any leaves at all. The white paper blew in every direction like a tornado was coming through. It was a sight to see!

When we were almost done, the cops turned the corner, blue lights flashing. Some neighbor had likely called them to stop our antics. Did Holly and I stick around? No, of course not. We ran like our lives depended on it, through the back yards of other homes until we could sneak safely back in Holly's house. To this day, our parents are unaware of this incident.

HEALING PART 6

Finding Your Purpose for Your Pain

There's a reason you've been through what you have experienced in life. In some way, you are called upon by the Universe to help one person, thousands, or millions with your story. Here's an exercise to find your gifts. This is a video many have used on YouTube from Pastor Craig Groeschel. If you are atheist or agnostic, I encourage you to do the exercises and take the God references out of it.

https://www.youtube.com/watch?v=5iyrf6TXrAc&list=PLLGY3cP0Rhtx-otxqKjNLfqdv9f2AEyk9k

HEALING PART SEVEN

Building Each Area of Your Life for Abundance

There are five areas of life on which I like to focus. These are the primary areas on which most people concentrate:

Health

Wealth

Peace

Purpose

Love

Health refers to your physical well-being. How does your body feel? Are you having health problems? Do you need to make seeing a doctor a priority?

Wealth can refer to finances, family, and friends. How is your financial situation? Are you struggling to pay the bills? Do you have a retirement account started? Would you be secure about the future if you were to lose your job? Do you feel like you are surrounded by people who are supportive and loving? There is so much to unpack here.

Peace refers to your everyday mindset. Do you wake every day feeling like the Universe has your back? Do you let things that would bother most people go because you know you didn't cause it, you can't control it, and you can't cure it? Have you learned to let toxic people go with love?

Purpose speaks of what your reason for living is. What is your purpose on this earth? Is it to teach men and women that they can overcome abuse and live a joyful, peaceful life? Is it to teach young children how to love each other and build strong relationships of their own? Is it to bring more people to your higher power? Is it to help children who are orphans? We all have a purpose. The Chazown lesson above has hopefully opened your eyes more to your reason for living.

Love is just love. It is both all-consuming romantic love and the love we feel for our kids. Do you have love in your life? Maybe you didn't receive healthy love from a parent, but have you found it elsewhere, in another person who stepped in to be Mom or Dad?

Most of my clients struggle in the areas of wealth and finances and love. It's easy to find yourself in credit card debt or overextended on a house or car payment. And love is right next to financial issues. We all want love, and true love is rare. But it is there for you to find or for it to find you?

Here is an exercise that I want you to do to evaluate where you want to grow. It is difficult for all five areas of life to be hitting on all cylinders. We usually struggle in one or two areas.

Take out a piece of paper and rank where you are the strongest to the least strong. For example, a client of mine did this:

1. Health (she is healthy but wants to eat healthier)

2. Peace (her spiritual life is strong, and she practices yoga)

3. Purpose (her mission is to help women recover from physical abuse)

4. Wealth (she needs to pay off her credit card debt soon)

5. Love (she went through a tough breakup with a narcissist last year and is now healed and ready to find true love)

Now, ask yourself what you can do to grow each area of your life. For example, as soon as I recover from my detached retina surgeries, I will be back in the gym to lift weights. I also need to eat more clean foods on the weekends instead of so much Tex-Mex. So, I will put these goals down under "health."

The trick to meeting any goal is to take baby steps. Maybe I will eat Tex-Mex only on Friday nights and not on both Friday and Saturday. That's how I will start my progress toward that goal.

Other Parts of Your Healing

Healing isn't linear. You will find you have days where you feel like you can conquer the world, then you'll have others where you feel like it would be better to stay in bed. This is a normal part of healing.

Also, I don't think we ever finish healing. Maybe Mother Theresa finished healing in her later years, but I can't think of anyone else. Fully healed would mean being at a place of 100 percent peace all the time, no matter what life throws at you.

I encourage you to find a counselor and a coach, too, if you can afford it. You will likely keep one or the other throughout your life. It is good to have someone invested in your well-being. My counselor and my coach are my cheerleaders. After what I have been through, I need people in my corner to encourage me to keep going and reach for my dreams.

Find online support groups for whatever trauma you have been through. One of my favorite groups is Victorious Voices on Facebook. I started this group four years ago to help survivors of narcissistic abuse. We give each other advice out of love and respect. My admins delete snide comments, and the person is removed from the group, although this doesn't happen very often. If you need this group, you can find it here: https://www.facebook.com/groups/197673434312459

Other groups my clients have found helpful include Daughters of Narcissistic Mothers, groups revolving around aging parents, Daughters of Alcoholic Mothers (or Fathers), and more. Keep your eyes open for a group that will be based on this book. I'll announce it on all my social media platforms.

CHAPTER 6

CHANGING YOUR MINDSET TO FIND YOUR PERSON

DATING STORY #6

"Cornhole Man"

A few years ago, I dated a guy who was a ton of fun to be around. Chris was always laughing and eager to do something fun, even on a Monday or Tuesday night. Chris was also intelligent, handsome, and successful, yet I don't think he understood how to relate to me or another busy woman.

One evening, Chis took me to a cornhole tournament. If you haven't played cornhole, you might enjoy it. You can play it almost anywhere, and it's popular at football game tailgate parties.

Cornhole is a game involving two or four players, bean bags filled with corn, and two platforms, each with a giant hole in the center. Official cornhole rules on USCornhole.com say the boards are placed twenty-seven feet apart.[13] The object of the game is to get as many bags as possible through the hole. Each team takes a turn, and hitting the hole is one point. Players keep score, and the first team to make twenty-one points wins.

Anyway, I spent the night watching Chris play his game. It was hot and sticky out (welcome to a Texas summer), so I amused myself after the eighth game by meeting people and drinking beer. By the end of the night, I was a little tired of bean bags, mosquitos, loud music, and little attention from my date. I guess it was an important cornhole tournament.

Anyway, I got an Uber home and called it a night.

Later the next week, Chris called me at 8 p.m. and asked, "Do you want to meet me out in a few hours for a birthday party for a girl I know?" It was a Tuesday, and I had a fourteen-year-old son at home. There was little notice, and I had to travel the next day. I explained to Chris that I preferred a day's notice so I could plan. The next three invitations were the same, and then the fourth said, "I hope I run into you out sometime soon."

Um . . . no.

Finally, I got a real date invitation a few weeks later. Chris texted me, "Would you like to come watch me play cornhole tomorrow?"

I responded, "Can we go now? I can't wait. What an honor!"

No, I didn't really say that. I said no, thank you.

Lesson learned: I discovered I didn't want to date someone who couldn't respect my wishes. Sure, being last minute is often fun, but I have responsibilities and want someone who wants to see me bad enough to plan. I reminded myself not to take it personally. He obviously needed someone at his disposal to watch him play his favorite game, and I was clearly not his girl. We just weren't a match. I do hope his team wins the cornhole championship.

Your Mindset Matters

Your mindset matters more than anything in dating and in life. We attract what we believe we are, and we become what we believe and tell ourselves. Guess who talks to you more than anyone else? You. The voice in your head is the loudest voice there is, so it's important to make it a supportive, loving, and guiding influence day after day. Here are some principles on how to navigate the dating world while having a strong, healthy mindset.

Why Emotions Can Rule Mindset

The parts of our brain that can affect our emotional state and our ability to reason are the amygdala and the frontal cortex. The frontal cortex is the control center of the brain, which regulates emotional expression, problem solving, memory, language, and sexual behaviors. This is the area of our minds that says, "Not so fast" or "Slow down" or "It's okay." The frontal cortex doesn't mature until a person is twenty-four to twenty-six years old. This is evident in most teenagers, especially boys, if you watch them over time.

The amygdala is the larger part of the brain, near the back of the head, that affects emotions. When we allow the amygdala to take over, we are making decisions based on emotion. In trauma survivors, this can be common. As someone who has been through years of trauma, I am aware how my amygdala often jumps to the fight or flight response when I am feel like I am in a dangerous situation. I am learning to slow down and ask myself questions like, "What's the truth here?" or "Is this really dangerous, or am I being triggered from the past?" When we are angry, sad, crying, anxious, happy, or euphoric, we need to stop and listen to the frontal cortex. Sometimes we may need to take a time-out for a few hours so we can calm down and hear what the frontal cortex is saying.

Let's look at some examples of when the frontal cortex takes over and when the amygdala rules the day.

An example of how the frontal cortex isn't mature or engaged in the teenage years was fully evident last July. My teenage son and his buddies thought it would be fun to bring inside what they thought was a dud firework. Guess what? It was live. The Roman candle didn't have a bad fuse after all. At this point, they panicked and shoved the firecracker under a bean bag, where it blew up. Styrofoam and feathers moved like a tornado in the room, making it difficult to see your hand in front of your face. The boys, still not thinking, heaved the burning chair out the window. Their reasoning went out the window, literally. The amygdala was in control.

Another example of when the frontal cortex is engaged is when my friend went car shopping. She wanted to trade in her twelve-year-old SUV for a newer, smaller, German-made vehicle. Susan did all the research, including finding out what her trade-in value on the SUV should be and what monthly payment was affordable. The car salesman tried to sell her on other options that would entail Susan blowing her budget. The nicer car toyed with her emotions (amygdala), but her frontal cortex said, "No." Susan still got a great deal and a new car because she listened to her reasoning and told her emotions to step aside.

Mindset Tip #1: Embrace Being Single

My Aunt Lulie once told me, "There are a lot worse things than being single."

Learn to love your single season. Where you are today doesn't determine your forever. Rich Wilkerson Jr. wrote in his book *Single and Secure; Break Up with the Lies and Fall in Love with the Truth* that "Being single doesn't equate to being stuck." Wilkerson also said that being single is a blessing, not a problem. Wilkerson mentioned the prophet Jesus in these words: "Jesus was single, and he changed the world."[14]

Unfortunately, society doesn't see being single as a season or blessing but more like a scarlet letter. For decades, culture has projected shame onto those who don't have a partner. Some of this is a generational stronghold from the early 1900s when men and women were expected to fill traditional gender roles. Women were supposed to marry young, have babies, and take care of the home. The man was the partner who worked to make the primary salary for the household on which the family could live. With this model, society began to impose on people that being married is a requirement for happiness. Today we know it's certainly not.

There are many single people who live great lives. They determine their own journeys, from work to travel to love. They aren't struggling to fit in with an outdated stereotype by marrying just to be married. These strong and single men and women don't feel the need to be rescued. They know love will happen if they set themselves up for it. It won't be required so they fit in or so they have happiness.

Personally, I did love being married and will enjoy it again, perhaps soon. In fact, I love men! However, I want to make the crucial decision of whom I marry out of love, not pressure and societal or cultural expectations.

Many times, I've witnessed an insistence that something is wrong with me because I'm not married. Like many of you, I could have been married three times since my divorce, but *the person wasn't right for me.* Why make a life-altering decision from what others expect? Unfortunately, marriage proponents don't listen to my voice and that of other singles.

Society puts enormous pressure on people to fall in love and have a significant other, even a second or third time around. To add fuel to the fire, friends and mere acquaintances ask me, "Are you dating anyone?" These people often mean well, but some want you to find a partner so you can share their relationship complaints or join them on double dates. Also, there are those people desperate for a relationship because they can't be alone. They don't care if it's with a soulmate or someone who is more like a roommate. Relationship addicts see me and other happy singles living their best lives and it scares them. It prompts them to look in the mirror and ask the difficult question, "Am I happy in this relationship?" It's more comfortable for many people to insinuate others need to partner up rather than admit their relationship is unhappy or toxic, and they need to make a change.

Is the Ring Really the Win?

If you are a woman over forty, growing up in the '70s and '80s likely meant your family and society taught you that you weren't considered whole until you were married. Even for younger women, you may feel this pressure if your family still believes in marriage as the ultimate prize and destination. A marriage proposal once told the world that "I am worthy and enough now. I have a man!" Sadly, that still happens today. Many young people get married because their friends are or they want babies, only to end up in single season again because they rushed and didn't vet properly.

Sure, there were dating games in the '70s and '80s in the deep south. But get this: there were also board games that taught little girls to daydream and fantasize about marriage. One such game was manufactured by Selchow and

Righter Co. and called "Bride." The goal of the competition was to become the first bride by making your way around the board and collecting something old, new, borrowed, blue, and the list goes on. This game today might be labeled misogynistic and archaic.

Unlike the game, I believe that being married is not the goal; being happy and at peace is the ultimate prize. If that involves marriage and kids for you, great! It did for me, too. I wouldn't trade my son for the world. I loved being married but not to the person I entered that union with. That relationship deteriorated quickly because I didn't vet, and I wore my love goggles. For the first three years I didn't take them off. Ever. Then, reality ripped them from my face, and I woke up to a difficult divorce. I felt like my end goal had moved, but I didn't know where.

So, let's not make marriage the end of our lives. It's not a destination or a "win." Let's look at marriage or a monogamous, serious relationship as something sacred and important that can happen during our journey. It's not the end of the road. We win by living with peace and joy. Yes, marriage can compound the happiness we already feel, but it's not going to be the only thing that will bring it.

Divorce in the '70s and '80s

I grew up in small town America, where some people would point at a single woman and refer to her as "That divorced woman." In fact, my parents told me when I was ten or eleven that I couldn't go play at Jill's house because she was "from a broken home." There was an insinuation with many married people that bad things happened at broken homes. To set the record straight, I am not criticizing my parents. This was a common phrase of that generation, and they knew nothing different. It's what their parents taught them. And hey, parts of this mindset are correct. There's seldom anyone who can always get a single mom's back. Recently, when I was working out of town, my teenager wanted to see how many of his buddies could sleep over. I returned home to half the varsity boys' basketball team sleeping on every soft surface available. The pantry was decimated. The refrigerator held only vegetables. But everyone was safe. (Cameras were still installed the day I came home.)

Let's remember that we don't know what others are going through in a divorced family. Maybe the wife emotionally abused her husband. Perhaps the husband physically hurt his wife. It could also be that one of the partners gambled away the equity in the home. Such judgment doesn't belong today, yet people still criticize. We're a quarter through the twentieth century, and you don't have to listen to those denigrators. Out of personal experience, I can tell you I am whole and happy after my divorce. Prior to that, during my marriage, I was a shell of what I am today. Divorced or single doesn't mean broken. Many families are more solid than ever with one parent at the helm.

Mindset #2: Marriage Can Help Happiness Grow but not Jump-Start It

A study published in the *Journal of Happiness* in 2017 found that marriage may make some people happy, but a legal union is no guarantee of happiness.[15] Researchers John Helliwell and Shawn Grover gathered subjective evidence from married and single people. Those that scored the happiest were people who had married their best friends. This leads me to believe it's not just marriage than can provide satisfaction, but the bigger issue is having a friend by your side when life grows too difficult to handle alone.

Anecdotally, I know several people who are not married to their best friends, and in fact, they grow farther apart each year. These are the people whose lives appear perfect on social media, yet Mom and Dad have slept in separate bedrooms for two years, and each partner is having, at the minimum, an emotional affair with someone else.

Comprehensively, the study showed that married people are happier than single people but not by much. Some singles in the study were significantly more at peace and more joyful than a married person the same age.

Bottom line is that we are wired to have connection and relationships, whether of the romantic kind or friendship. That's why depression and anxiety rates grew exponentially during Covid. Few could have the connection they craved. Being online during the pandemic was a stopgap, but there's nothing like having a conversation in person followed by a giant hug from a friend or lover.

During this single season, go out and have a blast!

During this single season, go out and have a blast! We are old enough to decide that if we don't want to do something, we don't have to do it. If it makes us happy, we can embrace it. If you want to travel, learn to make sushi, open a yogurt shop, go to a country concert, watch a professional football game, or run a marathon, do it. Don't wait on your Cinderella or Prince Charming to live your best life. Go live that life *now*.

And guess what? When we are happy, we attract people. Don't lose sight of who is running next to you or sitting by you at the concert. You never know who you'll meet on your journey living your best life.

Mindset #3: It's Not About You

It truly isn't about you. You've done the hard work to dig through your past and put the pain behind you. You have invested your time and effort into being the best you that has existed. Be proud of yourself. So, when a date goes sideways, understand it isn't about you.

Not everyone has focused on their healing journey. They just want someone like you or me to appear and fix things. To hurt people, we are giant Band-Aids. Hurt people often carry the pain from one relationship to the next, because they never fully recover from the previous relationship. It's simply adding layer upon layer of pain. If one person can't make them feel better, they think the next one will.

Let's look at reasons someone may not need to be dating but is anyway. These are reasons a date may not go the way you had hoped, but I give you these to remind you it isn't about you.

- They are having financial problems.

- Their ex-wife is asking for more child support.

- Their dog or cat just died.

- They are also taking care of elderly parents in addition to four kids every other week.

- Their job is in jeopardy.

- Their best friend just died or received a fatal diagnosis.

- Their car is in the shop, and Uber is expensive.

- They just broke up with someone and have no reason to be dating.

- They are starting a new job and can't afford to buy you a drink, much less dinner.

- Their sister moved in, and they don't get along.

- Their vacation got cancelled.

- They aren't over their ex.

- They are tired from working two jobs and should've stayed home.

I hope you see where I am going with this. Does any of the above have to do with you? No. Not at all. And you may meet some people when dating that are going through something like this. It's. Not. About. You.

Mindset #4: Actions speak louder than words

People can talk a big game. Men I've dated have promised me a week on a 170 ft. yacht in the Caribbean and a few days in Napa. Others have vowed to seek counseling or improve their quickly declining health. Did any of these things happen? The trip to Napa did. And that's it.

Men and women eloquently pronounce their plans for the most amazing relationship you will ever experience. But you must ask yourself: do their actions follow?

Actions mean more than words. Always.

Mindset #5: Learn to trust yourself

One of the most difficult things to do is learn to trust yourself. This means listening to your body, your emotions, and what your energy is telling you.

First, it's important to hear what your body is saying to you. If you are around a person and you feel anxious or scared, ask yourself, "When was the last time I felt this way around someone?" It may have been the last time you were around a person who lied to you. Experiment with your body and its message. Stick around for a few minutes and see if this person is a liar. Or leave and know it's better to miss out on a good person than to get stuck with a liar and cheater.

Many of my clients report feeling butterflies when they are around narcissists. However, they know from experience it is difficult to discern between butterflies from attraction and anxiety from walking on eggshells around a toxic person. Stop and listen to what your body is saying. Take a time-out from that person, meditate, and listen to yourself.

When I am around toxic people, my stomach clenches, my heart races, and I feel lightheaded. I know this is how I react when I am around a narcissist or another toxic person, so I exit stage left to safety every single time.

I also have had the same gut-wrenching reaction when an ex-boyfriend, a covert narcissist, was sending me texts. Just seeing his name appear in my inbox stressed me out, so I blocked him.

Also, listen to your feelings. Does being around a certain person or group make you sad or anxious? Listen to what your feelings are telling you. Would you feel better leaving? Then leave. You must protect your peace.

Finally, listen to your emotions. From pain to frustration, your emotions can be a flag that something is wrong. If you are frustrated with someone or a situation, then that's your body and mind saying, "This isn't right, and you need to address it." It's healthy to make small decisions based on emotions, such as skipping an event because you are sad about your parents' declining health. But be careful about making big, life-changing choices. Emotions, when overwhelming, can cause us to make major changes, from filing for divorce, screaming at a stranger, or calling the police on a neighbor. Do your best not to make major decisions when you are in any emotional state, even happiness. Don't get married in Vegas after dating for three weeks because it's convenient and sounds fun, and by the way, you love your dress.

Mindset #6: Therapy isn't just good for you . . . it's great!

Don't be ashamed to talk about dating with a therapist or coach. Dating in today's world can be difficult, and it's comforting to have someone who watches your back with making partnership choices. I often talk to my therapist about many relationships, especially about the person I am dating. Sometimes, love makes us put blinders on, and we can't see the truth right in front of us. Find a good, honest therapist who listens and guides you through dating choices. They can see what you need and what you don't, even when you can't.

For example, my therapist is a great guy named Dr. Shawn Lee. One afternoon, after I had been dating a man for some time, I thought I was seeing a red flag. The man I was in a relationship with was extremely focused on clothing and especially vocal on what I should wear when we went out to dinner or a concert. Like many women, I tried telling myself I could deal with such control, but my intuition told me differently After being married to a narcissist who manipulated with high control and low empathy, I saw a big red flag. My therapist congratulated me on seeing it and calling it what it was: authoritarian and unhealty. Then, Dr. Lee reminded me that my boyfriend's culture often labeled women as subservient and the man as the one in charge. Dr. Lee helped me dodge a bullet.

How to Reset Your Mindset

If you feel like online dating can be exhausting, you're not alone. Endless swiping and having the same introductory conversations over and over can be grueling to the psyche. Perhaps you spend time and think through great introductions for every match, yet in return you get a "WYD?" That means "Whatcha Doing?" I would love to respond one day, "Not you." Anyway, I digress. Dating can wear you out if you let it.

There's data to also back up the feeling of exhaustion from online dating. Single Reports is a team of data scientists, statisticians, and researchers who are passionate about the singles community and the data that drives its interactions. Singles Reports did a recent survey of men and women that revealed that four out of five or 78.37 percent of singles felt emotional fatigue or burnout from online dating.[16]

The emotional fatigue and burnout can be linked to spending hours swiping with little to show for it at the end of the day. Sometimes there are matches, and sometimes there are none. Also, as I mentioned, sometimes you get a half-ass reply (as my dad would say) or you don't get a response at all. It can be disheartening and make us want to throw our phone and its apps out a moving car window or delete everything relationship related.

That's why it's crucial to put boundaries in place when it comes to your mindset while dating. Here are some guidelines and suggestions that can help.

1. Set a daily time limit for online dating.

It's easy to start swiping and get lost in the search. I call it going down the rabbit hole. Set a time limit and check your messages at breakfast, lunch, and nighttime or just morning and evening. I think thirty minutes is ample time for each. That's an hour out of your day! When I am using the apps, I set a time limit for ten minutes. I find I am happier this way.

2. Take a break when you need it.

When you get tired of the short responses, manifestos, and basic bull s$%*, then take a break. When you are looking at online dating like a chore, take a break. The energy we put out in the universe will come back to us in many forms, and you don't want your discouragement, sadness, frustration, or anything else to come across in your messages. Take a week or a month. Whatever you need. What's meant for you is for you, so don't worry about missing out on the perfect person for you.

Laura's wisdom: What we chase runs away from us. Think of a cat. Let it happen. A break doesn't mean you're giving up, but it means you are recharging.

What we chase runs away from us.

3. Understand that you're not alone in this.

Just like the survey of five hundred men and women discovered, most people become emotionally exhausted and burned out during the dating process. That's the critical time to take a break and come back with a fresh mindset.

4. Remember that there's a light at the end of the tunnel.

We are going through all this for a reason. You will find your soulmate and your forever. But you won't find this person if you are negative, frustrated, mad, and sad all the time. Millions have found love through online dating or dating the second, fourth, or eighth time around. Don't give up. They're out there waiting for an amazing person like you.

Laura's wisdom: If you believe in a higher power, such as I am Christian and believe in God, ask your higher power for help. I often pray for discernment and energy as I go through the process. I often ask Him to guide my steps and teach me what I need to learn to be the best person for my husband that I know is out there.

Here are my daily reminders:

I will protect my peace at all costs.

My love or attention is valuable.

My time is valuable.

I am the bomb.

I am beautiful inside and out.

I am worthy of love.

I am enough!

If their absence brings me peace, then I didn't lose them. They lost me.

If my intuition tells me it's true, I need to listen. No excuses.

CHAPTER 7

RECOGNIZING RED FLAGS

When all you know is fight or flight, red flags and butterflies feel the same.
—Cindy Cherie

DATING STORY #7

Surgery Man

When I walked into the sports bar, the music was just loud enough to give the place a great vibe on a Saturday evening. College football was on every TV, and my Razorbacks were playing and winning. My date was sitting at the bar for our first meeting, and he looked like his pictures. What a great night, I thought. This has potential!

The conversation flowed well for the first half hour as we talked about our teenage sons and their antics. Then, the discussion turned to working out. This guy, Ronnie, was very fit and big, so I knew we would have a lot to talk about. I am a walker and runner, contingent on any injures, and I shared that with him. What Ronnie said next was a red flag.

"I am having hip replacement in six months," he told me. "I had it scheduled, but my girlfriend of many years and I broke up in the spring. I had no one to take care of me. So, I rescheduled the procedure for the first of the year because I think in six months, I can find another girlfriend to take care of me after surgery."

Um . . . no.

"Are you looking for a girlfriend or a nurse?" I asked him.

The date went downhill from there, of course.

Sure, we may have events, procedures, or trips in which we want or need a plus one to join us. However, I am not a believer in revealing that on the first date unless the upcoming event is a fun concert, adventure, or other outing. This guy wasn't joking, and I have enough on my plate as a single mom for this to be revolting. Had I fallen in love with him, I would've been more than ready to help him through a tough surgery. But this guy blew his chances with me.

Red Flags

There was a time I looked at red flags and thought they were beautiful. These colorful banners were a sign for me to work harder to change or fix this person. Now, I see red flags as warning labels for pain, hurt, and betrayal. Red flags that you overlook in the beginning will be the same reason the relationship ends.

How many times have you looked at someone and thought, "Wow, she has great potential?" Or maybe you met someone and thought, "He just needs some guidance on how to speak to a woman. I bet his mother never taught him this, but I can teach him how to treat me well. He has never been appreciated or been with a woman like me." My response to these thoughts is, "Um . . . NO."

No matter how much we work to help someone change, it's not our job.

No matter how much we work to help someone change, it's not our job. Without their desire and devotion to altering their personality or actions, it isn't going to happen. Yes, they may promise us that if we stick around, they will be able to change more quickly. Or they may beg, "How are we supposed to work on things when we are apart?" Deep down, we know the answer. Even though most people (if not all) are broken and damaged in some way, abusive behavior is abusive behavior. Throw the reason out the window. The abuser in the relationship needs to do some work, while the recipient likely needs to work on being codependent and allowing the abuse to repeatedly happen. Yes, we can be victims, but it is our choice how long we remain victims.

My guess is you may have already been to counseling during an abusive relationship to see what YOU could do to save it, when most of the destruction of that relationship wasn't due to you at all. The biggest thing you did detrimentally was to yourself when you didn't walk away the first or third time your partner emotionally, psychologically, or physically abused you. I know it's one of the hardest decisions to make, but so many of us have stayed years or decades longer than we should have in an abusive relationship. I certainly have. It's like moving from a dark and stormy sky to one with rainbows and sunshine.

Use past relationships as lessons as you begin your new dating life. There's an adage that I've proven correct too many times, much to my embarrassment. "Fool me once, shame on you. Fool me twice, shame on me." Each time that I have gone back to a relationship for a second chance, I have been deeply hurt.

Other Ways to Avoid Red Flags

Avoiding red flags may involve keeping friends and family out of your dating life. Everyone has opinions, and you don't want their guidance to derail your gut instinct, do you?

For example, when I was with my long-term, abusive partner, I had many friends and some family tell me, "Laura, he loves you, but he doesn't know how to show it." Or "You need to love him more, give more, love him harder." (What???)

I've also had well-meaning friends give me terrible relationship advice. When I was felling low, unloved, sad, hopeless, and more, some friends would say "keep going" when the best thing for me was to stop, regroup, and rest. I always felt better after a good night's sleep.

One of my church mentors asked me one day why I was taking advice from a certain person. Jonathan, my friend, said to me, "Why would you ask her for relationship advice? Her life is a trainwreck. That's like a physician asking a landscaper for a second medical opinion for a patient."

Point taken.

The Two Biggest Red Flags

Before we dive into what narcissism is, let's look at two of the biggest red flags that will eventually destroy a relationship. The first is contempt, and the second is a lack of empathy.

1. **Contempt.** Contempt is the feeling that a person or a thing is beneath consideration, worthless, or deserving of scorn. Psychologists around the world have studied contempt, and a few have determined that contempt is the biggest harbinger of a relationship that won't last.

   Drs. John and Julie Gottman founded the Gottman Institute. They were the first psychologists to look at the Four Horsemen of the Apocalypse. This is a metaphor depicting the end of times in the New Testament. They describe conquest, war, hunger, and death, respectively.

The Gottmans used this metaphor to describe communication styles that, according to their research, can predict the end of a relationship. The four horsemen are criticism, contempt, defensiveness, and stonewalling.[17]

Contempt is destructive because where criticism attacks a person's actions and character, contempt takes a position of moral superiority over a person.

I often listen to people speak about their exes, and when I hear them degrade that person and talk about how they were always the better person in the relationship, a warning light goes off in my mind. No one single person is ever responsible for the ending of a relationship.

Red Flags That Indicate Narcissism

As many of you know, I have published two books on narcissism after being in relationships with narcissists for forty-four years. I know narcissism and its aftereffects inside and out. If there is one piece of advice about dating a narcissist, it's this: RUN.

Narcissists are out to destroy you. Narcissists consistently, and I mean always, present with actions that facilitate insidious side effects. They are out to harm those closest to them, especially you.

Narcissists have a mental health disorder or personality disorder. There is no cure, and many psychologists will tell you the same. Dr. Lundy Bancroft is one of those. Dr. Bancroft authored the best-selling book *Why Does He Do That; Inside the Minds of Angry and Controlling Men*.

Dr. Bancroft counseled approximately two thousand men over two decades, and the psychologist said only a few changed. The ones who changed worked hard on altering behaviors and controlling their rage. They did this work through support groups, couples counseling and individual therapy. Personally, I don't like the odds. Bancroft reported that only a few changed.

That's a rate of about 1–2 percent. And those people didn't change their core personality, heart, or soul. These abusers changed only their behaviors.

I have heard Christian women say, "God can change him." Yes, many believe God is omnipotent and can do anything, and He can. However, I believe the person who needs transformation must be receptive to the thought of a higher power and His instruction. Narcissists often believe they are the higher power, and therefore will not truly accept that a person, idea, or a spiritual being is a superior. Why should they change? Narcissists get everything they want through their actions.

Traits of Narcissism

There are nine traits of narcissism listed in the Diagnostic and Statistical Manual of Mental Health Disorders, Fifth Edition, or DSM V. This manual is the written authority for psychologists and psychiatrists as they diagnose mental health disorders. Narcissism falls in the category of Cluster B Personality Disorders.

The DSM V states that if a person exhibits five of the nine traits listed below, the person should be diagnosed with narcissistic personality disorder, or NPD.

1. A grandiose sense of self-importance

2. Preoccupation with fantasies of unlimited success, power, brilliance, beauty, or ideal love

3. Belief that he or she is "special" and unique and can only be understood by or should associate with other special or high-status people or institutions

4. Requires excessive admiration

5. Has a sense of entitlement

6. Is interpersonally exploitative—takes advantage of others

7. Lacks empathy

8.   Envies others or believes others are envious of him or her

9.   Shows arrogant, haughty behaviors and attitudes[18]

I'll break these down by the biggest red flags indicating that someone may be a narcissist.

First, narcissists often display high control and low empathy. Watch how a person is around their parents, children, animals, and people who can do nothing for them, such as a server in a restaurant or a clerk at the grocery store. Toxic people often make unrealistic demands and speak down to others.

In fact, many narcissists believe they can only associate with or speak to people who are special or high status. Narcissists believe there is a societal pecking order, and they need to be or reside at the top. The next time you invite a person to an event, and that person questions you about the status, beauty, or monetary worth of the people attending, watch their actions closely. If the event doesn't meet their standards, they likely won't go, or they will exit stage left quickly. I had a narcissist once tell me, "Let's make a cameo at this party; then we can go where we really want to go."

Narcissists also carry a sense of entitlement and require excessive admiration. If a narcissist walks into a meeting or social situation and people don't flatter them or grovel, narcissists will be the first to leave. Narcissists expect others to be jealous of them or intimidated by them.

Narcissists take advantage of others, too. Narcissists often steal from their own families or workplace because they believe they are owed that for whatever reason. Many also lie and cheat often, as they feel they are entitled to as many lovers or as much sex as they desire. Narcissists have little remorse or repentance, which makes cheating and lying easy for them.

Some narcissists will discard a partner or lover only when another one is previously lined up. Narcissists need narcissistic supply, and that comes in the form of many things: attention, admiration, money, power, and unlimited sex Many narcissists also collect various beautiful people because they see people as objects, not human beings. On the professional front, narcissists often hold jobs or receive promotions they didn't earn.

Finally, more than anything else, narcissists need control. This sense of power protects their identities and fragile egos. Most narcissism originates in childhood because of biology and environment, so a narcissist learns early on how to manipulate people to satiate themselves. They learn or develop tactics to get what they need to survive. These needs don't stay fulfilled explaining their quest for more and more supply. It hurts for a narcissist to have down time because pain and feelings of inadequacy surface. Sadness and brokenness are deeply rooted in these people, despite their Teflon exterior.

There's a subset of narcissists that are called "covert narcissists," and they are much more difficult to spot than overt narcissists. These men and women often enter relationships undetected, their evil and controlling nature concealed by their actions and words. Here are some of the top traits of a covert narcissist:

1. Covert narcissists mirror you.

A covert narcissist slyly learns what you want and need with subtle questions and observation, then they give that to you. If you love being outside, they do, too. If you attend church each Sunday and pray before meals, guess what? The covert narcissist feels so lucky that they've met you! You understand them like no other!

Of course, this behavior stops or becomes intermittent when they realize they have hooked you. Then, your needs for being outside or attending church become too much for them to bear. The real person is beginning to emerge.

Covert narcissists are pathological liars.

Pathological lying is the chronic or compulsive behavior of habitually lying for no reason. Sometimes we all may tell a white lie to avoid hurting someone's feelings, but the narcissist's way of altering the truth is almost sinister. Many covert narcissists (CNs) tell so many lies that you don't know what to

THE NEW TRUTH ABOUT DATING

believe, and you must rely on them for the truth in every situation, because you now live by their truth as they define it.

Many times, this is an obsessive tactic to whittle down your self-esteem with lies or to alter reality to fit the covert narcissist's wishes and desires. Some examples might be, "My ex-wife used to wear heels in bed and sex me up before each business trip." In reality, this person's ex-wife traveled more than her husband, and they were seldom intimate because the marriage was so tumultuous.

2. Covert narcissists dismiss you.

CNs often dismiss your thoughts and ideas as if they are preposterous. Maybe you had an idea for your child's birthday party that you thought was great. The CN might laugh at you and tell you that you're an idiot.

CNs also don't listen or pretend they don't hear you. If it's not important to them, forget it. No matter how much you try to persuade them, their decision stands.

3. Covert narcissists are passive aggressive.

Have you ever been around someone, and you say to yourself, "Surely this person just didn't say that?" If that person is a covert narcissist, they may do a lot of that. They have no filter and often tell people things that are considered rude or condescending. Then when you question them about it, they dismiss you with, "You're too sensitive" or "I didn't say that."

Manipulative tactics used by narcissists and other toxic people

Gaslighting. Gaslighting is a buzz word today, much like narcissism is. Gaslighting is when a person attempts to alter your reality. These toxic people want to whittle away at your ability to see the truth, which makes you more dependent on them. You adapt to their version of reality. Here are some top gaslighting phrases:

- Stop making things up.

- Stop being so dramatic.

- I was just teasing/joking.

- Why do you always have to pick a fight?

- See, I can't even have a rational conversation with you.

- You're just jealous.

- Stop overthinking everything.

- You're just being paranoid.

- You need help!

- Everyone thinks you're crazy.

- No one likes you; you just think they do.

- Do you really think I would do something to hurt you?

- Stop exaggerating!

- I was just being nice to him/her. Can't I be nice?

- You are the problem; I want this relationship to work.

- You are remembering it wrong.

- We talked about this. Don't you remember?

- I didn't say that.

- I find it impossible to deal with someone who doesn't trust me.

- I criticize you because I love you.

- That never happened.

Triangulation. Triangulation is when a toxic person brings a third party into the relationship or discussion. For example, a harmful partner may say something like, "My ex-boyfriend was a great cook. It's too bad that you can't cook like he did." The comparison is intended to damage the self-confidence of the partner, so the partner works harder to be a better cook, lover, financial supporter, or whatever the case may be.

Triangulation can also occur when one partner brings a child or children into the mix. The toxic partner might say, "Little Suzy told me your boyfriend is really mean to her," when Suzy said no such thing. Such statements accelerate arguments and often break up a budding relationship.

Word Salad. Word salad is when one partner brings up a topic for discussion, yet the other party changes the subject immediately to avoid talking about what needs to be discussed. For example, maybe one person wants to talk about a recent bank statement or finances. The toxic partner might say something like, "We can talk about money, but first we need to talk about how you are raising the kids." When this happens, the controversial issue is never discussed. The toxic partner once again gets away with something usually damaging to the relationship.

Baiting. I've seen this happen with many clients and their toxic partners. Narcissists and other toxic people deliberately provoke you so that you emotionally react and swallow their blame-shifting. You believe it's your fault that an argument has ensued. For example, a toxic person might pick and pick at you, until finally you explode. Then the toxic partner says, "See, I can't even have a civil conversation with you."

Passive aggressive comments. These are comments that can hurt you to the core. A toxic partner may say something like, "Well, you're getting better at cooking, but this meal wasn't fantastic." Or you politely decline a date with someone, and they say, "Why do you always have to be so angry and bitter?"

Silent treatment. The silent treatment is a form of passive aggressiveness. It can last hours, days, weeks, or months. One client's boyfriend recently gave her the silent treatment for four months. Yet, when he was in public, he was consistently the most charming and talkative person at the event. As soon as they were driving home, he would become silent again.

The silent treatment is a message to tell a partner or person that you don't mean enough to me for me to even address you. You are nothing.

Hot and cold games. These games are the addiction-withdrawal games. One night a partner may dote on you and make you feel like you are the only man or woman in the world. The next day, the toxic person may not speak to you. The trouble is the healthy partner usually hangs on, waiting for the "good" version of a partner to resurface. This version usually reappears after longer and longer periods of time. This is how trauma bonds are developed. We wait and hope for the best version of that person to reappear, but this person doesn't exist.

Love bombing. Love bombing occurs at the beginning of the relationship with a toxic person. The unhealthy partner showers the victim with attention and affection. Often the toxic partner will text and call until the healthy partner is left questioning the sanity of this person. The toxic partner will push for physical intimacy early and often say things like "You're my soulmate" or "I love you" on a second or third date.

The unhealthy partner is also watching and listening to everything their potential victim says or does. They want their new target to feel comfortable and safe with them so they can learn all their secrets. The narcissist or toxic person makes note of these confidences, only to use them against the target later.

Devaluation. This is the part of the cycle that comes after the love bombing stage is over. Once the target is hooked, the perpetrator will eventually begin to say little things that leave the target questioning if they heard that correctly. The victim has been groomed to expect only love from her new squeeze, but now there's invalidation of almost everything she was told in the beginning. It leaves the target unsure of where they stand in the relationship. The target then begins to work harder and harder to win back the toxic person's love, which can never happen because it wasn't there in the first place.

Rage. This is the third stage of the abuse cycle. Many narcissists and toxic people have anger simmering just below the surface. You never know when they will lose control and their temper. Therefore, targets walk on eggshells constantly around a toxic partner. The unhealthy partner tells or intimates to their prey that their anger is a result of something they did. It's always the target's fault. Again, the target tries to appease the toxic person, doing whatever it takes to calm them down.

Hearts and flowers stage. This stage comes after the rage. This is when the narcissist or toxic person gives an empty apology and promises that it won't ever happen again. Often the toxic person promises to change if the victim will just stick with them. This stage is when targets get stuck. The apology, no matter how empty, gives the victim relief and a hope that there is change just around the corner. Yet, the cycle occurs repeatedly, often for years or decades. The target's hope seldom dies.

Empty apologies. I learned once through a therapist that a healthy apology sounds something like this: "I am sorry. I was wrong. Will you forgive me?" Toxic people are skilled at meaningless apologies. Their apology statements sound like, "I'm sorry, but you know how to push my buttons." Or someone may say, "I'm sorry that you are too sensitive." With this person, you will never get an authentic apology. They may do something that really hurts you, but it will be your fault. Toxic people take no responsibility. It's always someone else's fault, particularly yours.

Being the victim – This comes with people who are narcissists or others who just love attention. When something isn't going their way or they've been the perpetrator in a situation, you can watch them suddenly become the victim. "I only threw the chair in the pool because you made me mad," they'll say. "I know you will never love me, and it makes me sad. If you loved me, I would behave better."

Or maybe you say no to a simple request that you don't have time to fill. Your potential partner says, "Why do you hate me so much?"

These people will always be the victim, even when they did the crime. Your words or actions cannot make someone respond a certain way. Someone's response is *their choice*. Run. Don't look back.

7 Stages of a Trauma Bond

Let's be specific about how a trauma bond develops during the cycle of abuse with a toxic person.

1. **Love bombing** – As I stated above, this is what hooks the targets of toxic people. The predator (I use this term because a narcissist or other toxic person has carefully chosen their target. They see things in you or me that make us easy to manipulate and control.)

   Love bombing makes a target feel pursued, special, unique, and deeply loved. This stage can feel like a fairy tale. You feel like Cinderella or Prince Charming, and you are infatuated and not going anywhere.

2. **Dependency** – Gradually, a toxic person will make you feel dependent on them. There will be subtle intimations that you aren't quite up to handling a certain project or appearing at an event. There's a caveat though. If you let the toxic person help or attend an event with you, then you are capable. All your beliefs of being an independent person are fading away. You begin to question yourself because the person you initially met would never call you incompetent. You tell yourself they didn't mean it.

3. **Criticism and comparison** – This stage is when you begin to feel the first solid shift in the relationship. There's no second-guessing your partner's comments or facial expressions. Their behavior hurts and you ache for the person you first met to reappear.

4. **Gaslighting** – Once you are already losing self-confidence and self-esteem, then a toxic person begins to gaslight you. They tell you things that aren't true about yourself or those around you, but they

add just enough truth that you believe them. You begin to doubt your actions and your reality. "Maybe they're right," you think. "I can't do or say anything right. I am worthless."

5. **Resignation** - You begin to let the narcissist or toxic person define your reality by controlling all that you do. You are scared you'll mess up again, and they'll leave you.

6. **Loss of self** - You have lost all confidence in yourself. It's easier to rely on the toxic person for everything, without an argument. You don't want to be abandoned because you feel like you don't matter. Who would want you now?

7. **Addiction** – This push and pull and good and bad is called intermittent reinforcement. Your partner gives you a compliment and support one day, then for the next week tears you down emotionally with criticism or the silent treatment. During the good times you're ecstatic! You think that finally the difficult part of your relationship is over, and because you two have survived this, you can survive anything! This happens until the next day when the mask falls off again.

There's no reason or schedule to the madness. You never know what this person will dole out, so you hold on tight and hope for the good. Now, my friend, you are addicted to this person. Unless you realize the pattern, you will be a hostage to their moods and the relationship.

Other red flags that may not be narcissism

Money hungry- These are potential dating prospects who talk about money all the time. They may equate people's worth as human beings to the amount of money they make, the car they drive, or the private jet they own. Again, run. You will only be a dollar sign to them, even if you earn less than they do. One day it might be your fault the family doesn't have that new house because you won't change jobs. Or your partner will only want to go to events where rich people go. OR, the worst, your partner tries to keep up with the Joneses and you find yourselves in excessive debt. Your relationship will be transactional because people like this see everything as a possession to have or to criticize and throw away.

Future Faking – This technique is used when a man or woman wants to hook you quickly. Future faking is when a person lies or promises something about your potential future to get what they want in the present. It could be as basic as promising that they will call you later, and then never calling, or it could be painting a picture of your retirement together then ghosting you when things go sideways, usually because they cause the problems in the relationship.

I dated someone off and on for two years, and he was skilled at future faking. One evening, we were at his home, and he began showing me pictures of beach towns where we could retire together in the next decade or so. We both love boating, so he mentioned that all the places he researched were equipped with boat docks and waterway access to the Gulf or the Atlantic Ocean. A few months later, this guy told me he needed to explore his options and date different women but wanted us to continue dating each other. That didn't work for me. I can't "be serious" with someone, then go backward to friends or casual dating. No thanks.

Isolating: They only want to be with you, and while that might sound flattering, they also encourage you to cut ties with friends and family. This is a way for them to monopolize your time and attention. Isolating you also keeps you from people who can help you see clearly. You need a support system. Don't let anyone drive a wedge in between you and the people who matter the most.

Smothering: They constantly put you or others down, even if they mistakenly believe they're just kidding. This is one of the oldest tricks in the book. A partner wants to put you down to control you or prompt you to improve on something in the relationship. They say something in a way that's hurtful, yet when you confront them about it, they say, "I was just kidding." No, they weren't. And even if a partner was teasing, why would they continue to do it when it hurts your feelings?

All work all the time: Their job takes precedence over your time together, and they don't hesitate to cancel dates or leave you early to attend to what's more important to them. You will always come second to their work and the power they believe comes with it. Sometimes, you might find a double standard during the employment conversation. Their job is important enough to miss birthdays or anniversaries, but if you miss a significant event for work, then all hell breaks loose.

Affection-taking: They withhold affection or punish you by withholding affection. They will take all the love and attention you give them, but when you need a listening ear or a hug, they are nowhere to be found. Or, even worse, they are distracted when they are right in front of you. They don't even notice your tears. You deserve better.

Selfish: The plans you make with them only involve what they want to do, and they always get their way. If you suggest an event or restaurant, then they say "next time" or laugh off your suggestion. If you don't mind them being the one in control of almost everything you do, then you can date this type of person. Sometimes, I like to make my own choices, even if it's a small choice like having chocolate chip or rocky road ice cream.

Avoiding: There are important subjects that they refuse to discuss. These people don't like conflict, so they try to dodge difficult conversations at all costs. You won't be able to discuss finances or anything else that matters to you.

All-consuming: They say they love you right away, and even if you're not there yet, they don't back down. They want to book every minute of your free time, while you haven't even decided if you want to date them. It only matters that you satisfy their needs.

I think the bigger issue here is that someone wants to move so fast in getting into a relationship with you, that you don't have time to vet them or see their faults, nor have they been able to find yours. I know you are amazing, beautiful, smart, and kind, but they haven't had enough time to discover all you offer. They may be insecure, and you'll find yourself feeding their low self-esteem every minute of the day. Watch out for this one. Go slowly.

Ever-changing: You're never good enough, and they're always trying to change you.[19]

Self-hating – These are the men and women who often complain about their own actions. For example, maybe a woman grumbles that she drinks too much and even pours vodka early in the morning most days. Be quiet and listen to this person. You may learn what you need to learn before the second date.

Or perhaps a man complains that he doesn't know where his paycheck goes, and can he please borrow some money? Um, no. Give that guy nothing unless it's a budget for him to follow.

Too mysterious or goes MIA – These are people who often disappear physically or through technology. For example, my friend Tracy said goodbye to her boyfriend of a few months one Sunday morning. Around 3 p.m., Tracy sent Michael a text to say hello. She didn't hear anything back. Then she sent more texts at 5 p.m. and 10 p.m. Still no word. Her last text begged for Michael to tell her he was okay because she was ready to call area hospital. She heard back from Michael almost twenty-four hours later. His text said, "Good afternoon, love." Seriously? If you encounter this type of behavior, run the other way. Later we found out that Michael was also "helping a divorced woman through a tough time." Here's the translation: Michael was sleeping with someone else, and he couldn't text or call for almost a day because he was with the other woman.

Research shows that most Americans check their phones every four to seven minutes. When someone disappears or doesn't return your texts or calls for twelve to twenty-four hours, that's a red flag. Where is this person? Are they with someone else? Were they simply busy? It doesn't matter. People make time for what matters to them. If you are dating someone like this, kick them to the curb.

My thoughts are these: If you can go to the bathroom, you can send a text. Sit on the toilet, do your business, and text your partner. It takes only a few seconds.

I once dated a guy who sent every call but work calls to voice mail. There was never a text or call notification that appeared on his phone. Later in the relationship, he would leave his phone in the office when we went to bed. Sometimes I would wake up, and this guy would be "working" in the office because he couldn't sleep. Really? I was gullible and thought he really had insomnia. Later I learned that he was juggling several different women. We all thought we were his girlfriends. Again, actions speak louder than words!

Your potential partner lives at home with Mom or Dad

This doesn't necessarily have to be a red flag, but you might want to investigate. Is your love interest living at home to take care of a sick or elderly parent? That's admirable. Or is it because your potential partner can't hold a job or spends all the money he makes on child support or partying? Does their parent cover the rent or house payment? If the answer is yes to the last questions, and you desire a partner who is independent, I would think about moving on.

Most importantly, there's an overriding question when it comes to moms and sons. While many men have a special relationship with Mom (which is awesome), you must ask them in a subtle way, "What does it mean for you to cleave from mom or dad? What does that look like for you?" Personally, I want an independent man who can pay the bills without assistance from Mom. I also want a self-governing partner who doesn't need to call Mom for advice every time an important or insignificant decision needs to be made.

I was at a friend's house recently, and her adult son called six times. The first time was a question about laundry, the second was a question about who he should date, and the third was something about grocery shopping. There's a point when we need to ask ourselves if a child simply misses the parent or if the constant contact is a form of codependency.

Still Can't Decide If it's a Red Flag?

Time or a crisis reveals character. Some people wait to be certain, so they watch the person's actions for a few weeks or months to be sure. If someone is toxic, they cannot keep the mask on forever. In my experience, the limit of the façade is two years. By then, the mask will fall off and you'll have your answer. It's exhausting to play the part of someone who isn't the authentic person, so take a deep breath and give it time, if you think this person could be worth it.

Often, a crisis will happen, and you'll learn someone's character. Maybe your car breaks down and you need a ride. Does this person come to the rescue? For example, I had a sad calamity a few years ago when my cocker spaniel died. I was a slobbering mess, and I couldn't meet Jason, the person I had been dating, for lunch. However, Jason appeared on my doorstep forty-five minutes later with flowers and a box of tissues, and he listened to me cry. I think I still owe him for his dry cleaning. His shirt absorbed a bucket of tears.

Don't forget, however, a red flag is a red flag. If you've seen it, it's not going to disappear. The red flags you see now will later lead to the destruction of the relationship or you.

Frustration

For instance, how does a partner handle frustration? We all get frustrated at one point or another. For an emotionally healthy person, frustration can indicate that something is off-kilter and needs to be altered or adjusted for a better outcome. For a toxic person, frustration can ignite anger, rage, feelings of injustice, or the desire to get revenge on the perceived perpetrator.

Grief

How does a partner handle grief? There are no guidelines for grief. Psychiatrist Elizabeth Kubler-Ross determined that people go through five stages of grief. These are: denial, anger, bargaining, depression, and acceptance. It's important to remember that the process isn't linear. You can't compare your grieving to someone else's mourning.

Where this comes into play in romantic relationships is like this: Does your partner take out his anger from the loss on you and others? Does this person then take zero accountability for their actions? These are questions to ask yourself about a potential partner. In every relationship, there will be grief. It could be the death of a parent, pet, or child. It could also be the grieving of a past relationship. Grief is part of life. How does your potential partner handle it?

On a positive note, I've seen many relationships where the couple respects how the other partner grieves. I remember one man who needed time alone to process the loss of a loved one. He would tell his wife, "Hi sweetheart, I am going into my cave now, but I'll be back."

Listening – Some people are great listeners, and some aren't, yet they try. How much do you need them to listen? I am hoping some, because if you don't have an emotional connection with someone, it's going to be difficult for the relationship to grow. A lack of an emotionally intimate relationship will also cause pain when one person is hurting and the other isn't there to help. Many times, it's simply because they don't know how to be a good listener. Can you teach someone to listen? It's probably one of the simplest techniques to teach a person who authentically wants to grow. Listening doesn't mean fixing. Sometimes men and women just need an ear or to know someone cares.

Celebrations – Some people are all about how things look and not the substance of interactions. For example, does this person plan elaborate celebrations only to post the events on Facebook or Instagram to show the world how special they are? Or does this person genuinely think about the celebration and plan according to what those involved want? Is it about emotional connections with loved ones or how it looks to the outside world?

Yes, it is possible to throw an epic party or event where everyone has an exciting time and enjoys each other. It's important to recognize the true motive, however. Was it an IG friendly event? Did the hostess take fifty-eight pictures, only to post one? This type of event exhausts me. I crave authenticity and realness. If you do too, then watch for those who are more interested in "likes" than whether they bond with a relative or friend.

Birthdays – Narcissists in particular love to ruin birthdays or any event that makes others happy. They believe all the happiness in the world should be theirs. And if they see someone else experiencing joy, they want to take it. If you experience someone deliberately trying to ruin your birthday or another special event, watch their actions carefully for a few weeks. Do they have your best interests at heart? I have withheld painful information so I didn't ruin friends' birthdays. Unless it's crucial, bad news can wait twenty-four hours.

Money – Is money the most important thing to them? Is your money their money and their money is their money? Stinginess in finances can translate to miserliness in emotional support and love.

Time – No matter how busy someone is, if they want to make time for you, they will. No one is that busy.

Friends – Does your potential partner like your friends? Have they at least tried? If those people are important to you, can your partner understand your need to see them? Do you need to have a serious conversation about their control?

Also, what do your friends say about your love interest? Is this person accepted or ridiculed? Or are they silent so they don't hurt your feelings?

THE NEW TRUTH ABOUT DATING

Where There Is Extreme, There Is Error

Is a person you are catching feelings for extreme when it comes to something? Money, alcohol, sex, their kids' sports, or religion? Where something is extreme, there is usually error. Something is missing and that person is trying to fill a void. Be careful.

Prior love interests - We've all had them, so leave them where they belong: in the past. End of story. Don't mention them to hurt your partner or to make them jealous. Also don't bring former lovers up for any type of comparison. All of us want to think we are the best person that our new boos have met, and vice versa. Don't hurt the other person with stories of you and your ex climbing mountains or traveling.

Phones – I saved the best for last. A partner's phone can be a window into their life, even one you didn't know they had. You can see how past relationships evolved and crashed, how feelings are expressed to others, and what they carry deep in their soul. I understand no one should ask for phone passwords or access at the beginning of the relationship. I wouldn't want a potential partner knowing that I was texting my best friend about my upset stomach the night before.

However, there are clues that surface during everyday interactions that can give you an idea of what exactly is going on in their phone and in their life.

Remember the first dating story I told you about? It was about a guy from Austin who was a chameleon. My friend Holly and I called him "Lizard." My gut often told me something wasn't right, especially when it came to his phone. I would see him placing his phone face down anytime he let go of it. Also, he would take calls in the middle of the night ("I am talking to London, baby. I'll be right there.")

There were other times I would call him, and my calls or texts would go unanswered for hours, if not a day or two. If you recall from Chapter One, Lizard often sent them directly to voicemail. A friend of mine said she had dated a CEO before, and that type of person is typically married to work and barely has time to eat, much less make a phone call. I thought to myself, "It takes five seconds to send a text that says, "I love you" or "How's your day?" For example, my seventeen-year-old son sends texts sitting on the toilet. Embarrassingly, he will also FaceTime his buddies from the potty. People can find the time to text if they want to be in contact.

I could've saved myself a lot of heartbreak if I had watched his behavior with his phone. I had seldom heard him talking to colleagues from work. There was an entire world going on in that phone that resembled nothing that he pretended to be.

When you are serious about someone, there is a point in which you need have a conversation about phones, privacy, and transparency. Ask what your partner thinks, then be quiet. If your partner becomes defensive and angry about sharing anything on their phone, that's a red flag. Take a step back and watch what they are doing. If your gut tells you there's more going on in that phone than at a college fraternity mixer, listen to your intuition.

A phone can also reveal positive character traits about someone. Do they have motivational quotes that pop up daily? Do they reach for their phone first thing in the morning to pull up a devotional? Or do they text a child or an aging parent every night to say, "I love you"? This is good stuff. Don't overlook this either.

CHAPTER 8

FINDING A HEALTHY RELATIONSHIP

For many of us who have been in toxic relationships most of our lives, it's good to reinforce what a healthy relationship looks like. I know from my experiences with both toxic and healthy romantic relationships, great relationships are easy, especially in the beginning. Sure, there are some ups and down in a healthy partnership but nothing compared to volatile, toxic unions. If it's unstable and explosive in the beginning, what do you think the middle and end will look like?

If you were to draw a diagram of what's the bare minimum of a healthy relationship, it would look like a triangle, with the three points being these:

1. **Commitment**

2. **Emotional Connection**

3. **Chemistry**

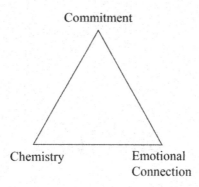

Commitment

Chemistry   Emotional
               Connection

Let's look at **commitment** first. This is a key part to a romantic relationship that will last. Both parties want monogamy and want to be committed to each other. In some cultures, or with certain people, a commitment or marriage may mean including others sexually or emotionally. But what is the bottom line? The two people at the core of the relationship want to be together. (I believe in monogamy, but some other couples do not. I have been asked on Bumble to be a third person in what a few couples call their healthy marriages. It's not for me, but I am letting you know what you may come across.)

For me, commitment means one man and one woman. It is defined for me as myself and a partner. We are committed to each other emotionally, intellectually, physically, and sometimes, in marriage, financially. At the minimum, we share house payments and bills.

We all know money can be a tricky thing when it comes to relationships. You do what you think is best with money, but I believe each partner needs to carry their weight. That can be either be earning money, taking care of kids, working outside the home . . . the list goes on.

Secondly, a healthy relationship needs to begin with an **emotional connection**. Men typically don't need this as much as women, but some emotional connection is needed to have a truly healthy, loving relationship. There must be agreement between the two parties in the romantic relation-

THE NEW TRUTH ABOUT DATING

ship. Maybe both parties like to take life lightly and just have fun. That's an emotional connection that works for them.

Finally, there's **chemistry**. This is the most elusive of the three. You will not have chemistry with most people, no matter how much you try. Sure, sex may be good with some people, but true chemistry is rare. It feels like a needle in a haystack. But when it's there? At the beginning of a relationship, you won't want to leave the bedroom.

Don't settle when it comes to chemistry, because chemistry often fades as a relationship progresses through the years. Why would you want to start at zero when you can start at a ten?

Markers of a Healthy Relationship

Once you have determined that you and your partner have an emotional connection, commitment, and chemistry, what's next? Below are markers of a healthy relationship. Both partners should have the traits below.

- **Acceptance** – Transformational Coach Dr. Dharius Daniels says, "If someone can't get over your past, they don't need to be in your future." I agree! This person may not agree with some choices you have made in your life, but they accept them and don't hold you hostage to your mistakes. And vice versa. Accept your partner and their past mistakes and victories.

- **Respect** – You respect each other's wants, needs, desires, values, morals, boundaries, and more. You may not always agree completely about something like religion or politics, but you respect that your partner has their opinion, and you have yours.

- **Trust** – You trust each other not to break the rules in your relationship. You are each honest. Neither of you hides things from the other.

- **Communication** – You decide how much you'll communicate, and you are open and transparent when you do.

- **Commitment** – You both agree on being monogamous or how much you are committed to each other.

119

- **Kindness** – You approach each other with sincerity and gentleness.

- **Enjoyment** – You have fun together and enjoy being around each other.

- **Support** – You support each other's goals and interests.

- **Decisions** – You make important decisions together, especially when the decision involves money, children, the home, and sex.

- **Feelings** – You both feel supported and cared for. You also feel relevant and understood, even if you agree to disagree.

- **Reciprocity** – One partner doesn't carry a heavier load than the other, even if the loads comprise different tasks.

Only you can determine your nonnegotiables. Some people are stalwarts when it comes to religion preferences. Others are determined to date someone who lives in a certain area because they don't want to move. For some, deal breakers surround financial independence or lack thereof. Only you know what your dealbreakers are. However, I do encourage you, if you meet someone you love but they have a "dealbreaker," to ask yourself tough questions. The first is, "Can I live without this person?" And the second is, "Is there a way around this dealbreaker?"

I'll give you an example. If you love to snow ski, and the woman of your dreams doesn't or can't, do you stop dating? Or can you ski half a day, then spend the rest of the day with her when on vacation? This is just a hint here, guys: I am guessing you would get some of the best sex of your life by doing this.

Finally, you don't want to miss the dating checklist in the next chapter. It covers most relationship pitfalls when there is no agreement or understanding.

CHAPTER 9

DEVELOPING YOUR DATING CHECKLIST

It's important to have a dating checklist. Here is one that I crafted after reading one from my former life coach and incorporating my own concepts. At the bottom of this questionnaire, you can also add your nonnegotiables. We all have them. Write them down, and don't be ashamed.

This is not a scored checklist but a list of questions we often don't ask ourselves. You must decide what is a dealbreaker for *you*.

1. Does this person have a healthy relationship with family?

2. Is this person involved with their children?

3. Does this person have more than one baby momma or daddy?

4. Has this person been married more than twice?

5. Is this person rigid with their beliefs and seldom open-minded about critical issues?

6. Is this person sleeping with anyone else? Is there a friend with benefits?

7. Does this person hold a regular job?

8. Does this person own or rent a home?

9. Does this person live with their parents?

10. Does this person take care of their health?

11. Does this person spend conservatively or frivolously?

12. Do this person's life goals match with yours?

13. Does this person give to a charity or volunteer time?

14. Does this person spend time alone with God or a higher power? Does that mean something to you?

15. Is this person overall a happy man or woman?

16. Does this person handle stress well? Do they drink a lot or do drugs? Do they exercise?

17. Does this person attend counseling?

18. Does this person want a long-term relationship? Does that match with what you want?

19. Do the friends of this person call him or her "a player?"

20. Does this person share your secrets with others?

21. Does this person get your back when people are after you or against you?

22. Does this person blame you for every problem in the relationship?

23. Do the actions of this person match their words?

24. Does this person treat animals well?

25. Is this person often rude to someone who can't do anything for them, like a server in a restaurant or store clerk?

CHAPTER 10

UNDERSTANDING DATING TERMS

All It Takes is One

Many men and women tell me, "There aren't any good (women or men) out there! I'll be single forever." It's important to remember it only takes one person to find your match. You might sift through or date hundreds, but there will be that one if you open your healthy, healed heart to better. With nine billion people on the planet, don't you think there's one for you?

Bumble says dating in 2022 and beyond is going to look a little different in response to Covid-19. Many singles found themselves isolated and lonely during Covid, but they were afraid to date due to the virus's unknown factors. Now these singles are ready to face dating head on![20]

Trends we might see in dating include the odd yet funny label of "oystering." No, it's not eating oysters on a date or looking for the rare pearl in an oyster shell. Oystering is facing the dating world head-on as if the world is your oyster. It's embracing your singleness and going after what you want.

Do you want to have a date five nights a week? Then go for it! Do you want to see a movie with a different person every Sunday night? Then make that happen. It's treating dating not like a chore but as a growth experience and a lot of fun!

Dating terms to know

Bumble executives have said that we will continue to see dating trends evolve or regress, depending on how we look at them. Here are some terms to understand in your own dating journey.

Ghosting – this is a term most people know. Ghosting is when someone stops communication without giving a reason. Even when the ghosted party reaches out to see what happened, they are met with no response. It's hurtful and demeaning. There are only a few times when it's warranted. We will discuss those in subsequent chapters.

Oystering – After the pandemic, many men and women are looking at dating as an exciting way to reenter the world of face-to-face meetings and conversations. Their mantra is, "The dating world is my oyster." Many of these people want to date as much as they desire and meet many people. It's the opposite of the days of the pandemic when the only people you saw were on Facetime or Zoom.

Dates without drinking – Bumble execs say they are seeing a trend of more dates that don't involve alcohol. Some potential partners are meeting at coffee or juice bars or for a walk through the park. It's not necessary to meet in a bar or restaurant any longer; just make sure you meet in public.

Ground hogging – This term describes dating the same person over and over but with a different face. We must ask ourselves how can we choose differently? What are the choices we are making that are poor?

Breadcrumbing – This the act of sending out flirtatious but noncommittal social signals (i.e., "breadcrumbs") in order to lure a romantic partner in without expending much effort. In other words, it's leading someone on. This technique is often used to keep someone around while deciding if there is someone else "better" to date.

Submarining – This is a form of ghosting where a person drops off the grid, only to resurface with a text or conversation months later. Sometimes it's just as you were finally getting over being ghosted in the first place.

Fast-forwarding – This is when a relationship moves at breakneck speed but crashes at the end. When things move too quickly between two people, there is often little to look forward to or anticipate.

Hey-ter – These are the people who start online chats or texts with, "Hey there." And sometimes, that's all they write. There's got to be more originality than that. Look up a new line if you need to or turn to Chapter 8 for some tips.

Pocketing – This is when a potential partner doesn't introduce you to family after a significant amount of time has passed. Are you a booty call? Start investigating.

Orbiting – These are the guys or gals who communicate with you regularly, then stop. They resurface quickly by commenting on your Instagram and Facebook posts. Yet, they never ask you out. It's someone who really isn't interested or is cowardly. This person isn't worth your time either way.

Whelming – These are the people who brag about how many matches they have on dating apps. They say these things to impress you, yet they dig a hole for themselves. Such conversation isn't warranted. It's arrogant and exhausting. My dog Charlie could have twenty-five matches on a dating app tonight if I created a profile for him.

Untyping – This is a trend where people go out with others with whom they never would have accepted a date before. It's dating someone who isn't your usual type.

Slow fades – A person slowly stops communicating with a prior love interest. They don't respond to messages as quickly, then they stop responding altogether.

Wokefishing - Ever dated someone who you think pretends to act "woke"? Well, they may be wokefishing you. The term refers to those who act as caring about the same sociopolitical issues as you in a bid to reel you in and date you, when it is all an act. Terrifying.

Negging - Negging the practice of giving backhanded compliments and generally making comments that express indifference toward another person (usually a woman). It's an attempt to seduce that person by being just of reach. An example is, "That's a great new haircut, but I would never have the courage to wear it." Or someone might ask, "Have you lost weight? You're starting to look good."

Catfishing – This happens when someone on a dating site uses old photos or photos that aren't their own. Catfishes may also lie about their weight or height, and when you meet them in person, they look and act nothing like their profile. This is another reason to meet in public or have a Facetime conversation before making plans at all.

My friend Amy is someone who I believe was catfished worse than I've been or seen. Amy swiped right on a man's profile whom she thought was handsome and not her usual type. She felt brave for branching out. The man appeared to be tall, dark, and handsome. He was a great communicator. However, when she met him in person, he was shorter than his profile indicated, 40 lbs. heavier than his picture, and of a different hair and skin color. It wasn't even his photo. It was an image he'd found online!

Amy called him out on it, so he bought her and her friends drinks the rest of the evening.

Kittenfishing – This is when people make themselves seem more attractive on dating apps by using filters, old pictures, and inflated profile descriptions. This could look like a woman who says she is "Assistant Vice President of Operations" at work when really, she is "Assistant to the Vice President."

Zombie-Ing – An ex as a zombie is an amusing thought, but it can also be traumatizing. And much like zombies, this technique is not an authentic reappearance. Zombie-ing is when a former partner who disappeared reappears after a few months. They typically text, "Hey, how have you been?"

The issue behind zombie-ing is that is sometimes the zombie truly wants to reconnect, but only for selfish reasons. The ex is typically feeling lonely or in a relationship that is going sideways, and they want the attention you gave them at one time. Sure, it can be flattering that they want a reconnection, but it's almost always short-lived. You are some type of supply for them, and when you make them feel better, they disappear again.

Cuffing Season – This refers to the fall and winter season, when single people seek companionship due to the wintry weather and holidays approaching. It's nice to snuggle by a fire with someone when snow is falling outside, or it's enjoyable to cook a big meal together for Thanksgiving rather than order takeout. These "cuffing season" relationships are usually short-term, fostered out of loneliness rather than true compatibility and attraction.

Freckling – Did you ever hear an older family member talk about a summer fling? That's called freckling now. Some people look for a short-term relationship to last the summer, so they don't have to go to warm weather concerts, beaches, trips, and more alone.

Roaching – This is a common relationship issue. This is when people are secretly sleeping with other partners. You may feel you're in a relationship

THE NEW TRUTH ABOUT DATING

with them, and they are with you, but the terms aren't defined. This word is assigned to such occurrences because it's like when you find one roach, you find a swarm. If you catch your significant other in being secret or seemingly not divulging all, call them out. They usually scamper like a roach. My general rule, which I learned the hard way, is that if the other person hasn't defined anything, then you are both free to date other people.

Caspering – Remember Casper the Friendly Ghost? Casper was the pleasant, personable, and translucent ghost in animated television shows and films. Just as Casper could fade away, so do these potential partners. They may regress from texting you every day to once a week to every few weeks to never. That's okay. Keep it moving. Their loss. You don't want to be in a relationship with someone who isn't sure, do you? I don't.

White clawing – This is when people hold on tight to someone else just because of their dazzling good looks, even though the person is boring and a terrible conversationalist or basic communicator.

Situationship – You are dating someone, and you have not defined the relationship. You could be exclusive, seeing other people, or just friends with benefits.

Friends with benefits – This means you are sleeping with someone just for the sex. There is no relationship beyond friendship. You owe each other nothing.

Other trends include "**hard balling**." Hard balling is when you tell your suitor what you want out of the relationship. Are you looking for casual? Then you tell the other person. Are you wanting something long-term that leads to marriage? You ask the right questions to see if that's what they want, too. Women, a side note for you here. If you ask a guy on the first date whether marriage is in his cards, clear the path for his exit. Such a question will scare away even the best, most monogamous men. I've seen it happen personally, even when I knew the other person was looking for his forever. Men like the chase, and I'll get to that in a minute.

Dating now may also take the course of dry dating or going on a date where neither party drinks alcohol. Some women and men meet for coffee or at a juice bar. I've met men for long walks in a (crowded) park. I am not saying there's anything wrong with meeting for a beer or other cocktail beverage. That's my favorite thing to do because it helps me relax. These are options that I am giving you to consider.

CHAPTER 11

DATING WITH INTENTION

Whether you are looking for something casual or a long-term relationship, this is the chapter to help you build a strong profile and navigate the dating applications and their algorithms.

Choose the site

Bumble - Bumble is an online dating application. Profiles of potential matches are displayed to users, who can "swipe left" to reject a candidate or "swipe right" to indicate interest. The difference between Bumble and other apps is that on Bumble, women make the first move. A man can swipe right on a woman he is interested in, but unless she swipes right back and starts a conversation, there is no match. All different nationalities and age demographics are represented on Bumble. The user simply specifies in what age group he or she is searching, and whether the user is searching for a man or woman.

I also like Bumble because it was started by a woman in Texas. The CEO, Whitney Wolfe, wanted to develop an app wherein women could reach out first. Bumble now has a hundred million users worldwide.

Bumble is free unless you want extra perks like seeing who swiped right on you before you swipe on them.

Tinder – Tinder is also an app that's used on smart devices. Tinder is also an online dating and geosocial networking application. In Tinder, users "swipe right" to like or "swipe left" to dislike other users' profiles, which include their photo, a short bio, and a list of their interests. In some cities, Tinder is known as the "hook up" app. It's more for people who want to date casual or a casual sexual encounter.

Tinder is also a "pay to play" app with different tiers of membership.

Match.com – Although Match.com was one of the first dating sites available, I think it's a site that digs deeper into people's wishes and interests. Personally, I think the website is easier to navigate than the app, but that's just me. Match charges a little more than its counterparts per month for use, but if you purchase a longer plan, it can be less expensive than the others.

eHarmony – One of my best friends met his wife on eHarmony. Once you pay a fee and sign up, the site asks you a series of questions that determines with whom they think you will be a good match. Then you receive matches daily that fit that profile.

Farmers Only – The site markets itself as a site to find a cowboy, cowgirl, rancher, or animal lover. It can be free but with different fee levels, you receive more matches and more benefits.

There are many other sites that you can research and try. There's Elite Singles, Christian Mingle, Plenty of Fish, Seeking, Zoosk, OK Cupid, and more. Do your research and see what you think will work for your personality and your budget. You aren't locked into a contract on them, so you can give different ones a try. Be sure, however, when you are done with a site that you cancel your subscription. Many renew automatically, and those charges can add up.

Your Profile

Before you sign up for a site, hire a make-up artist to do your hair and makeup and a professional photographer to take your photos. This is key to looking your best for your profile pictures.

If you can't afford a professional photo shoot, then ask a friend who is good with an iPhone to take some pictures of you. If you can borrow a ring light from someone who shoots videos or does a lot of Zoom meetings, that will help, too.

If a make-up person is too expensive right now, then go to the make-up counter at your favorite department store and get a make-over. Plan to purchase something so you aren't taking advantage of their time and tell the make-up artist you are having photographs made.

As far as clothing goes, choose one dressy outfit and a couple of casual ones. You need to have two looks for your profile. People will want to see that you can grab a taco at a food truck and look fabulous while doing it, or that you can rock a little black dress or the best "fit" for a night out on the town or a special event.

As far as color goes, wear what you feel makes you look your best. Don't wear any patterns or prints because those tend to play with the camera lens.

Choose one great headshot and one full length photo.

When you get your proofs or you're going through your phone pics, choose one great headshot and one full-length photo. That's what you will put up as your profile pictures. You don't want to put up any more than two or three because some people on the sites can be judgmental. The more you give them to pick apart, the more they will do so. I hate this part about dating, but it's the truth.

Other tips:

Ladies and gentlemen, no **bathroom selfies, please**. Some people have posted pictures from their bathrooms where it looks like a clothing bomb has gone off. Hairbrushes, wet towels, dirty clothes, and the toilet provide the background. Do NOT do this. I don't care how good you look.

- Also, ladies and gentlemen, unless you're searching for your forever on a dating app for hunters and fisherman, please **don't post a picture of you holding a fish or other dead animal**. We are past the days of cavemen bringing home food and women cooking it over an open flame. We have grocery stores now, some of which are almost a luxury experience with fully stocked counters of fish and meat.

- I know your kids are gorgeous, smart, funny, and kind, but **please don't include your children** in your dating profile. This is about you. Yes, the kids are an especially important, if not the most important, part of the rest of our lives. But, please be cautious and don't put their faces out there yet. There is plenty of time for you to trade pictures of children when you find that special someone. You never know when someone is a creeper. My son is incredibly special to me, as most of you know. I don't even introduce him to potential suitors until the person has "staying power." When I am serious with someone, usually after six months, only then will the guy meet my son.

- Also, I did a little research of my own, to see what happens when kids are included in dating profiles. I changed a picture on Bumble of just me on the beach in a white dress to and almost identical one with my son in it. Same beach, same clothes, and an extra person. Guess what? My profile got half the right swipes. My kid is amazing, but those looking at the photos don't know that. They see a teenage boy, and many may think I need a man to help me raise him. That is the farthest thing from the truth! I don't need anyone's help with my kiddo. We've been fine just the two of us for years. Like many of you, I want true love, not a babysitter.

Show pictures of your kids on your first date if you would like. Let the person see how amazing you are, and they will understand how great your family is, too. If you are having trouble with your children, take a break from dating and get them on the right track. Then, my friends, get back out there. Our kids are our most important assets.

Also, if the limit on the website is twenty-five photographs, **don't post twenty-five pictures, please**. That's a huge red flag that someone is a narcissist. We know you are handsome or beautiful, but remember, less is more. Why do we need to see twenty-five pictures of you, your home, your car, your hamster, and your high school track medal? We don't. Save those for your third anniversary.

Writing your profile

You will need a username. I have used "Laura" and "Lovelife345." I've seen names such as "Red Raider," "Cubbybear," and "Yourforever." (That's a little presumptuous, I think.) Use what you are comfortable with. I've come across some profiles of men who use a completely different name. They may be Bob, but they post a name like Regan or Larry. Sometimes people are just shy, or often they don't want others to know their real names until they begin chatting via the app.

The section about you can get tricky if you let it. But that's why I am here to give you guidance. Below, you'll find questions to ask yourself before you write your written profile that appears under your best picture and username. Spend some time here. This is the most important part of your dating journey after your photographs.

- What are the three things you want someone to take away from reading your profile? For me it was that I am kind, fun, and ready to find the love of my life.

- What are the top three adjectives that describe you? (Funny, ambitious, empathetic, silly, adventurous, caring, spiritual, and the list goes on.)

- What do your friends say about you? (Ask them!)

- Are you looking for casual or long term?

- Where are your favorite places to vacation?

- What is something very few people know about you?

If you are struggling with writing a few paragraphs about yourself, have a trusted friend help. You can also book a dating coaching session with me at any point in this process. Here is the link: https://charanzacoachingsession. as.me/

Here are some things to avoid when writing your profile:

- Don't be negative. At all. I have come across several profiles where the user seems angry about the dating process. Here is an example:

If you don't look like your pictures, then I will drink until you do. If you are a Biden supporter, swipe left. If your kids are under sixteen, swipe left because I am not raising anyone else's children. I am an empty nester, and I am looking for the same. Also, if you want a texting buddy, ask your eighth grade neighbor.

All I have to say is "ouch." That person is really hurting. Every phrase and description in that profile is negative. Swipe left on anything like this verbiage.

Here is an example of positive: *My friends say I am funny, smart, kind, and adventurous. As a former marine on the front lines, I believe in our country and its values. Since I am retired, my life now revolves around my grown kids, and I can't wait to focus on a special woman and best friend. I'd love to introduce you to my favorite vacation spot, and maybe you can help me learn more about yours.*

- Don't write too much. Don't reveal everything about yourself. It's intriguing to others when there is a little mystery.

- Please don't write, "Just ask me." If you cannot take the time to write a few sentences about yourself, then it seems you aren't engaged in this process.

Meeting people online

Now you're ready! Make your profile go live and jump in! Spend some time each morning or evening swiping and messaging. I find that delegating not more than ten to fifteen minutes twice a day keeps my clients from becoming overwhelmed.

Stick to your messaging schedule, otherwise you will drive yourself crazy. It's easy to wonder if someone has received your message or they are ignoring you or if you offended them. Get out of your head. We are all so busy. If someone doesn't respond, it's their loss. Keep it moving. You'll find three more interests who will.

Once you have a match, it's time to reach out. If you are on Bumble, ladies, you must reach out first, meaning you must write a message to that person. Other apps will allow either user to reach out initially. These apps, ladies, is where I want you to sit on your hands. Men need to send the first message if it's an option. Yes, it's old school, but it shows interest. If a few days go by and you don't hear from him, even though you've matched, then you can send something light-hearted about his profile. An example would be, "I see your wing man in one pic is that handsome dog. What's his name?" or "Where did you learn to surf? Great pic!"

After your message, let it go.

After your message, let it go. Remember it's the world of online dating. You may or may not hear back. DO NOT TAKE THIS PERSONALLY. This person could have been texting with someone they met weeks or months before you, and they've decided to focus on each other. Or this person you matched with is a player and likes collecting numbers and pictures. Either way, they aren't for you. KEEP IT MOVING.

Also, let's talk about "the texter." These are often lonely people who use dating apps for communication only. They have no intention of ever meeting. When I have texted with someone for over a week, I politely say, "Do you think we will ever get off this app and meet in real life? I would enjoy that." They will either answer and say yes or ghost because they don't want to put the effort into a meet-up or date. That's okay! Let them waste someone else's time. You and your time are too valuable for that.

Other communication tips

I am a journalism major and English minor, so I can't publish a book without a few writing tips about messaging.

- Keep it lighthearted.

- Don't talk about past relationships. If they ask, your answer is, "It ran its course."

- Mention something regarding their profile or picture. "Where was that great pic taken of you on the beach?"

- Emojis can keep things light and positive if you like to use them. "I went to the dog park today, and my golden retriever was running around like a crazy dog!" (Insert laugh emoji here.)

- End each communication with a question. "I really enjoyed your thoughts on that new movie. Are there any others you want to see?" PLEASE do this. People don't understand when the conversation hits a dead end. If you tell me all about your day and don't ask about mine, I am not going to share anything with you.

- Please don't respond to a message with, "Hey there, Thx." Or, as a guy wrote me once, "Yes, it's really hot out." Um, delete. If a person can't make time for a thoughtful response, then I am not far up on their list.

And that's okay. If you find yourself wanting to write something like that, then move on. See my ghosting rules below.

- If you don't want to miss a connection, and the time is expiring, use this: "It's great to connect with you. I'm boarding a plane/washing my hair/mowing my yard, and I will write more later!" or whatever your reason is for what otherwise might be a lame text.

- Men and women love feeling statements, such as, "I learned to drive a race car today, and it was scary yet exhilarating at the same time."

- If you end a couple of messages with a question, and the person still gives one- or two-word answers, move on. I would rather communicate with my dog Charlie then pull teeth like that. At least I get a few barks and a sloppy kiss.

When Do You Ghost?

There are a few times when ghosting is appropriate, in my opinion. When someone is abusive, mean, degrading, or threatening, ghost them. Such behavior is inappropriate and even scary. You can disappear on someone in the following scenarios:

- They begin to talk in a way you aren't comfortable with, and you've already warned them to stop.

- What they say is so outrageous and inappropriate the first time, you need to ghost and block them. You can't change people. I blocked a guy on Bumble who responded to my first message with a dick pic. My friend Michael argues this isn't ghosting, but it's protecting yourself from abuse. True.

- They submarine you, and you never know when you'll hear from them. Personally, I would delete this person because I am clearly a back-up plan. And I remind myself that they are missing out. Better dates ahead. You and I are no one's back up. Period.

- You haven't been on a date and this person is just not doing it for you or is sporadic in their communication. Consistency is key in a relationship. They can't even get texting right. Thank you, next.

- You've been on a date with this person and aren't interested. Despite kindly telling them you didn't have the chemistry you desire, they don't take no for an answer. Ghost and block.

- You need to take care of you, and your ex is toxic as usual. Ghost. Block. Move on.

Don't ghost in these scenarios:

- You've had a few dates and kissed or been intimate. You owe this person some type of goodbye. Again, if they are rude after your breakup, ghost them.

- You've met someone else. "It was great meeting you, but I had a fifth date with someone, and I am going to see where it goes."

- If a person clearly has deep feelings for you, don't ghost initially. Let them know you don't feel what you want to feel, and your decision is not about them. If they respond with an ugly tone or mean words, then let it go. Move on. They are hurt, and you don't need to be their punching bag.

- You've lived together. This has happened to people I know. Men and women both have come home and found that the significant other has moved out. The person who left then doesn't answer texts or calls. Unless the person left behind was an abuser, murderer, thief, or other evil character, there is no excuse. None. I can't imagine the pain for the person left behind.

- You've had sex. If the other person goes bat s**t crazy on you when you tell them it's over, then ghost. At least give a kind goodbye. You've cleaned up your side of the street.

The DATE

First date – Think of this as a meet-up and not a "first date." You can put pressure on yourself when you label this a "date." This is really an interview for the second meeting or date. Remember, this person is a stranger. You know little to nothing about them, so there's no reason to be nervous.

Also, meet in public for the first and second date. Meet at a restaurant, popular park, coffee shop, or ice-cream parlor. *Never go to someone's home the first time.* Trust me, this has happened, and it didn't end up well for a client of mine. Things can go south quickly, so it's better to have people around.

Keep it light during your first meeting. You can ask a few questions to get answers off your dating checklist, but this meeting is really to find out if there's chemistry and/or a connection. Don't put pressure on yourself to find more.

Ladies, I know this is where I failed many times early on. I would go from a picture on Bumble to walking down the aisle. True story. I would sit across from a guy to whom I was attracted, and before the date was over, in my head we were getting married. I learned to dial it back and to just have fun. Many men and women can sense when the other person is desperate. The energy shifts around the meet-up.

Now, I am more the heartbreaker than the one always left heartbroken. Why? Men and women both pick up on the other person's neediness. No one wants to go into a relationship where the other has preordained the future. Stop. If you are having a needy day or month, then take a break from dating. Or get your confidence up and make the date brief and remind yourself, "This is an interview. Nothing else. I am meeting a stranger right now and really know extraordinarily little about this person."

Second date – These are usually fun because you've both established you want to see each other again. Keep it light and continue to ask questions that pertain to your dating list. Don't ask about all the heavy issues, but sprinkle in two or three throughout the evening.

I'd like to add here if you aren't excited to go on a second date with someone, don't go. Don't waste their time and yours. If you think chemistry might develop or there's something intriguing about this person, then make the effort. I think we all know by the third date if there's a potential relationship in the cards.

Third Date – At this point, you both have an interest in each other, and it's time to still be cautious about what that means. There are some men who won't take a woman out on the fourth date if she doesn't have sex with them. If this isn't for you, then no loss here if he or she disappears.

Also, by now, I hope you've done a background check via one of the many websites available or through a private investigator in your hometown. Private Investigator Mike Duncan, a friend of mine in Dallas, has done a few for me when things were headed in a more serious direction. A hundred and twenty-five dollars can save you a lot of heartache or give you the confidence to take the next step.

Let's be positive though. Hey, when your date checks out, and you want to travel together later, go for it. You are ready to introduce this person to your kids in a few months? Go for it. Checking a person out isn't a bad thing. One caveat for you: Don't ever tell them. Don't tell your friends, either. This is your protection plan. Some people might think you are crazy, but why waste your time and safety going out with crazy people when it could be avoided?

If your budget is tight, then Google is your best friend. I was interested in a guy named Kyle early on in my dating days, and I Googled him. He had killed two people while driving while intoxicated. This was his fourth DWI. I didn't want to take that on after such a bad divorce. I am sure he is sober and doing well, but with my bad breakup in 2016, I was fearful of anything else causing me pain.

The Algorithm

This is an algorithm to get you started as you develop your own process in narrowing down your potential soul mates.

THE NEW TRUTH ABOUT DATING

1. **Online:** Communicate with no less than five to eight people online at any given time. You will get a good sense of someone's interest in you or lack thereof. Are you receiving short, one-word answers? Keep it moving. Are you having genuine conversations via messaging in the dating app? Then gather information. See my communication tips earlier in this chapter.

   If the other person doesn't ask to move offline to texting or a phone call after a week, you have a choice: You can stop communicating with this person, or you can say something like, "I hope we can meet sometime soon. My time is valuable, and I don't want to go on texting forever."

   Ladies, I let the man give me his phone number first. I've found if I offer mine first, some men think I am desperate. Men, don't be afraid to offer your phone number after several days or a week of texting. She may or may not text you, but you won't know if you don't try. If she doesn't text back, look up "Flakey" in Chapter 2 of this book.

First Meeting/Date - Look your best for the occasion. Feel confident, sexy, handsome, or beautiful because you are. This person is lucky you said yes!

Drop a few questions in from the dating checklist. Listen to their answers, and you can ask follow-up questions if you feel like it. Also, let them talk and ask questions, too. The conversation should be about 50/50 or 60/40, with them talking a little more. Most human beings like to talk about themselves.

Be authentic. Let's say you are meeting someone more conversative than you, and you change your personality to fit what you think this person will like. Guess what? This conversative woman or man is looking for someone with a little moxie and strong opinions. Now, your date isn't quite as interested as before. Be yourself!

In between first and second meetings – Ask yourself a few questions about the date.

1. Did I feel chemistry? Usually, a connection or chemistry is evident during the first few minutes of the first meeting. You can't miss it. If there's no chemistry, then remind yourself that you are one step closer to the person for you.

2. What did I learn from the date? Is there anything you would do better? If so, think about that for your next meet-up.

Ladies, if you do like the person after the meet-up, don't text. Let the guy text first. Men, ladies love to hear that you had an enjoyable time and will be in touch soon. If you aren't circling back, don't text her at all. Ladies, you'll understand where you stand with him after a few days away from the date. And if you don't feel a connection, it's okay to tell him that when or if he texts or calls.

Don't be a people pleaser and agree to a second date just because they check the boxes on paper. Sometimes the person can look like a perfect match, but the chemistry is back in the science lab at the local high school.

Regardless, keep dating others until the man locks you down. Do not zero in on one person. Let's keep a rotation on the bench until you know for certain who the number one player is.

Second date – Continue to ask questions that are important to you and continue to be yourself. If you are really into this person, have a date with someone else for the next evening or soon after your "right now" person. First, this leaves you being mysterious if they ask you out again soon. "I would love to do that, but I have plans tomorrow night." Always answer with a little mystery. Do not say anything about your health, stomach bug, or sick parakeet and that's why you can't see this person. You may be staying home to paint your walls, but they don't need to know that. That's too much information. You are important, busy, and valuable. Act that way.

Third date – You can hopefully have most of your checklist questions answered by the end of this date. Really tune in to how you feel when you are with this person. Are the butterflies from being nervous or something else? Do you miss this person when you aren't around them?

Personally, I think it's best to wait on sex. I know many women who have a third date rule. The longer you wait, the better it will be and the more mystery that will surround you.

Also, studies show that women think clearly about a relationship until they have sex with someone they care about. Men, however, think clearly after sex. Why muddy your waters until you learn what you need to know about this person?

Fourth date and on – Keep it moving until they lock it down, ladies. This could be after the fifth date or never. Men, you will know if you like someone enough to make sure she isn't seeing anyone else. Because if she's a catch, she probably is.

Let's trust ourselves on decisions of the heart.

Let's trust ourselves on decisions of the heart. When we ask our friends about whether we should be dating someone, they are giving us an answer from their point of view, holding their baggage they've had from previous relationships. If they're weary and tired from that, those friends might tell you to run from a great person. Learn to listen to yourself or to speak to a therapist or coach.

CHAPTER 12

APPLYING MY BEST DATING ADVICE EVER

This chapter covers my best advice about dating. If you have realistic expectations, this guidance will control your disappointment and point you in the direction toward the love of your life.

Not Everyone Is Honest

Let's circle back to Chapter 3 and dig deeper into what people are looking for when dating. A profile can read that someone desires a long-term (LTR) or casual relationship. However, even then, some people aren't honest about what they are seeking.

For example, there are some men I know who say they have the dating thing down to a science when it comes to getting sex from women. They often label themselves as a man seeking a LTR, yet they will date a woman until they have sex. Then, to really reel her in, they wait for a few weeks before contacting her or asking her out again. These men say this works almost every time. That way they have a roster of women to choose from.

What troubles me is that these men know what they are doing. It's a big game that ends up often with a woman hurt and the guy quickly moving on to the next victim. If these guys were being honest and saying they want casual and hook-ups, great. Many women would still bite. But the *perception* is that they are looking for something more.

I am not saying this happens with only men as the perpetrators. Women can be dishonest about many things, too. I know women who will only date men in a certain income bracket. They believe it's their privilege to be taken care of. They know where to go, how to dress, and how to seduce these men who have money. They go for the big fish until a larger catch comes along. But guys, if you wear your heart on your sleeve, I am warning you to be careful. As I have mentioned, go into any date or relationship with a nonjudgmental or neutral stance. Let the person prove themselves before you are vulnerable in any given way that may backfire and hurt you. You could find your heart broken and your bank account empty.

Understand Your Attachment Style

There's a best-selling book *Attached: The New Science of Adult Attachment and How It Can Help You Find – and Keep – Love*. This is one of the best books you can read about how you give and receive love. The authors, Rachel Heller and Amir Levine, explain why and how we carry attachment styles and sometimes trauma from our childhood into our adult relationships.

For example, if you were raised by a parent who was emotionally distant, made you work for love and attention, and was often critical, you may have an anxious attachment style. I find that in my work with sons and daughters of narcissists, this is the attachment style prevalent. Parents of these men and women often forced on their children their thoughts, beliefs, values, and morals. Anything else wasn't accepted. They applauded actions that shone the light on them as a great parent. These children had no one to nurture them, talk to them about their feelings, or simply listen. Only outward successes were applauded if they shone the spotlight back on the toxic parent. If this is you, you may subconsciously seek that in a love relationship. This is me. I used to only gravitate toward men with an avoidant attachment style because that's what I was most comfortable with. I wanted to fix them or work hard to make them love me. If I did not have to work for their love and attention, I believed the man wasn't for me.

The avoidant attachment style is just that. According to the authors Levine and Heller, avoidant people equate intimacy with a loss of independence and constantly try to minimize closeness. Signs that you or someone is avoidant may be that they send mixed messages, say they want a long relationship but hint it's not with you, or suggest that you are too needy or too sensitive. Other red flags that someone is avoidant are that they disregard your emotional well-being and provide little comfort for you and ignore things you say because they inconvenience them.

When it comes to dating apps, studies have shown that avoidants move on from relationship to relationship quickly, and they are in the dating pool for longer periods of time and more frequently.

Finally, there is the secure attachment style. People with a secure attachment style feel comfortable with intimacy and are usually loving and kind. Many enjoy sex and focus on its emotional component. They can clearly communicate their needs and expectations but in a warm and loving way.

What's most important to learn here is what attachment style you have and why you select the partners you do. For example, if you have an anxious attachment style, then when you date the healthiest choice for you, the secure person, you may find them boring. Personally, I did at first because I was so used to the drama that comes with dating a narcissist or other toxic person.

Understanding why you are attracted to certain people can change your proclivities and make your love life grow.

Stay Busy Being YOU!

The only person you can control in this dating journey is you. By staying busy doing what you love, you can take the pressure off yourself and make the process a lot more fun. Also, when you are being active in groups, in a sport, taking a music lessons, or whatever you adore, you aren't focusing on who has sent a message on the app and who hasn't. It becomes just another part of the day when you check your messages.

Know Your Triggers

Alcoholics Anonymous uses the acronym HALT when it comes to what triggers people to drink. HALT stands for hungry, angry, lonely, and tired. The same, can be applied to overanalyzing your inbox on dating apps. When you are hungry, angry, lonely, or tired, you may turn to your chosen dating app for some confidence building or attention. Don't do this. People seldom feel stronger, wiser, and more confident after getting on a dating app. That's because they are too many variables you can't control. People are busy, and the guy or girl you like may not have written you back, or perhaps that person has found a relationship elsewhere. When you aren't psychologically strong, this can make dating feel like a losing game. It isn't. If anyone is losing, it's the person who didn't respond to your message. Again, don't take it personally. Sometimes people get distracted by someone or something else. And if that's the case, you don't want them anyway.

When you are doing what you love and living your best life, your reaction will be, "Their loss." When you are home, bored, lonely, and tired, you may tell yourself wrongly that "No one will ever love me." I know this because I've been there.

Now, when I am hungry, tired, lonely, angry, or just frustrated with something else, I DO NOT get on a dating app. I go do something for me. The amount of self-care you need is in direct proportion to the degree to which you are feeling sad or damaged. Maybe phone a friend or go meet your sister for a walk. Take the dog to the dog park. Do something for you and no one else. The app and messages will be there tomorrow. If it's meant for you, it's for you, and no one can change that.

"Don't put all your eggs in one basket" – Grandmother Lucy Martin

My grandmother was put on a train at the age of sixteen in Birmingham, Alabama, to go to college on the East Coast. She was so intelligent that her high school graduated her two years early. The pitiful thing cried all the way up to Wellesley in Massachusetts. Despite her brilliance around math and many languages, I think some of the soundest advice I received from her was about men and relationships.

Grandmother Lucy married early. She met my grandfather Kenneth, while both were on horseback, on Grayton Beach in the panhandle of Florida. She was in the navy while he was in the Coast Guard. She would share stories about marrying my grandfather and raising my dad, who was super cute but still a hellion. What I remember most was when she said, "Darling, don't focus on one man until you know he's right."

Lucy was born in 1921, and her advice still stands. I know you may not like this when I say it, but date a lot of people when you are just dating. There are two reasons that I give this advice.

1. This stops you from getting hyper-focused on one man or woman.

2. You learn more about what you want and what you don't want.

When you are dating (notice I didn't say sleeping with) multiple people, you can look at your potential partners as a basketball team. When one goes on the bench, you simply replace that person with one waiting to play the game. This can go on until you find the special person who shows you with their actions that they are the "real deal." Then, and only then, can you clear your bench.

Also, by dating different people, you will learn more about many cultures, languages, values, and more. This helps you decide what you really want. Maybe you think you need a petite, tiny woman on your arm. Then you meet a gorgeous woman who is six feet tall, and she meets all your other qualifications. See? We can't help who we love, and if you keep yourself in a box, you might miss the best person for you.

I posted something in my online support group about dating multiple people to protect your heart. There was one member of the group that disparaged me for that. I was surprised. It's okay to casually date many people. I can almost guarantee 99 percent of the people using dating apps are doing just that. It's not forever, but it's until you find the right one.

I found this concept of dating multiple people in the controversial book *The Power of the Pussy* by Kara King. Women, I highly suggest you download the book or audible of this manuscript. It's fantastic. Men, many of you are already skilled at seeing a few women at a time. This is more for the gals reading this book, especially if you jump into every relationship headfirst, looking for love.

In *The Power of the Pussy*, author Kara King writes, "Men are like pots on a stove. How many pots can you cook at one time?"[21]

I am not saying date seven or eight at once, but at least have two with whom you are talking or texting. Please notice that I didn't say *sleeping with* but speaking to or dating. Why? Because when we get focused on one man too early on, we are more likely to mess it up. Really, you ask? Yes, because many of us are overthinkers. We can self-sabotage a relationship because we analyze one guy's every move. The guy may not be doing anything wrong, but if we overthink it, we can drive the relationship into the ground before it even starts.

For example, perhaps you had a date with a guy, and you felt like you clicked. He asked to see you next weekend, but he didn't set up the date. Don't overthink it. Go out with someone else. You may not know it, but maybe his uncle or cousin passed away and he's headed home. Or, in my case, I had race to Arkansas one Thanksgiving because my dad was having emergency surgery. Don't overthink. Don't grovel either. Just keep going. Meet another one, and if the one you are really interested in comes around, then great. If not, you won't know who you're missing out on if you don't try.

Not every man or woman you date has to be marriage material from the beginning. Enjoy meeting people of all nationalities and cultures. Date tall people, short people, big people, small people, beautiful people, funny people, not-so-pretty people, and serious people. The more men or women you go out with, the more realistic you'll be and the more you'll realize there are so many men and women to date.

I am emphasizing overthinking because I have wrecked a relationship or two by overthinking. Then I would come across as needy or insecure.

"I Need Space"

I have heard this many times and have said it to potential love interests, too. Sometimes I have uttered these words because I am not really interested, and other times I needed time alone. Sometimes work can be stressful, or a family member is sick, and well, we need a time-out. That's a smart move. When we are emotional, we can make bad decisions and hurt others.

However, there is a healthy way and an unhealthy way to take the time you need. It's not fair to someone to just disappear, then return with "I was in a bad place." You can take the same amount of time with love by saying, "I am having a difficult time and need to check out for a bit. Please understand that I'll be back." Or "I'll check in with you daily by text, but I am going to focus on work and feeling better right now. I want to be the best version of myself for you and others I care about."

This way, you aren't ghosting and doing damage to the relationship.

Stop Overthinking

This is yet another reason to stay busy and date many different people. When we are not occupying our minds with healthy thoughts, we can allow our brains to drift to the things we perceive that we did wrong on a date or even in our communication with someone.

Overthinking is also a symptom of someone with an anxious attachment style. And that, my friends, can destroy a relationship. When your potential boo thinks he or she is doing everything right, yet you are blowing up their phones with "Where are you?" and "WYD?," this sends the message that you need a lot of attention and well, babysitting.

Slow Down

Slow is fast and fast is slow. Think about that. Have you ever had a relationship that moved at lightning speed, and in two weeks, you found yourself in bed with this person? Then a week later, he or she just didn't seem interested? Yup. You moved too fast. Both of you did. The mystery was no longer a mystery. The fire had fizzled out. Slow down, because this person is still a stranger. You haven't gotten to know them. Also, you aren't supposed to know it's true love right away. Peel the layers off.

The longer you build the fire and the more logs you put onto it, the better the fire you make. It burns large and bright for a long time. Don't take it too fast. From the number of dates each week to how quickly you are intimate with this person, slow down. If they want sex and only sex, they will leave. If they like you for you, they will let you set the pace. Tell them you care and want to see where this relationship goes, but you want to learn all you can about them. The right person will respect that. They also have longer to imagine what it's like when they do get the cookie. Finally, it shows that you know your value. You won't settle for another drive-through relationship. You are worth much more than that, my friend.

You won't settle for another drive through relationship. You are worth much more than that, my friend.

Don't Share or Be Vulnerable Right Away.

I am an empath, and a trait of empaths is that we deeply need emotional connection with people. If the conversation feels shallow, I am ready to exit stage left. I feel like I have so little time to be around others, that I want to bond with them.

That said, I must hold myself back when it comes to sharing in new relationships. It is dangerous to be vulnerable with someone you don't know well. This person could laugh at your feelings or later use your secrets against you. Until you trust this person, don't share your deepest, darkest secrets. What if you tell them about the terrible year where you lost a family member, a favorite pet, and your job, and you don't see them again? How awful. You might feel like you left a piece of your heart behind.

Men Like the Chase. Really, We All Do!

My life coach, who helped me through healing after decades of narcissistic abuse, still talks about men and the chase. Rebecca Lynn Pope is a life coach and the star of the OWN television show "Marry Me." Rebecca hammered home to me that men inherently are hunters. They want to seek, find, and conquer. Therefore, it's always important to remain just a little out of reach. Keep them guessing.

For example, a friend of mine leaves her husband of five years guessing. Madison will sit in the car and have a conversation with me before coming inside at the end of the day. Inevitably, her husband will stick his head inside the garage and ask, "Who are you talking to, sweetheart?" Madison answers truthfully. But do you see where I am coming from? Madison still leaves a little mystery around her. Her husband must work a little to get her attention. This isn't a game. It's a strategy to keep your relationship interesting.

This can also work if you are a man trying to get the attention of a woman. I can't tell you how many times my guy friends have told me that when they back off from a woman they like, their phones start blowing up. A woman who once was the center of a man's world often can't stand it when he focuses elsewhere. They think, "What happened?" The nice texts and calls slow down or stop, and the woman is left wondering, "What did I do wrong?" So, guys, use this to your advantage when you feel like you've been overboard and shown too much interest. Go out on a date with someone else. Train your focus away from the one you think you love. Not forever, but so you can get some breathing room and come down to earth from your love cloud.

Being Accessible

This section is for both men and women. Don't be too available. Don't return every single message when your phone pings. Wait two hours but no longer than four to return a text. Remember that you're busy, and you're the bomb. You have a life to live. Focus on being technology free during some hours of the day unless you need your phone for work. And even then, put it down for a few minutes or an hour. Mystery is good. Be mysterious.

Also, I personally don't accept same-day invitations unless it's something I really want to do and have time to fit in my schedule. I find that most *people who seek last minute dates* fall into one of the following categories:

1. **Don't respect the time or schedule of others.**

2. **Aren't that interested but want some company for a beer or dinner.**

3. **Think everyone's schedule should fit around theirs because, hey, their job or kids are more important than yours.**

A Snake is a Snake

A snake is a snake. No amount of your love or attention will change that. The snake will always bite, leaving the venom behind to kill you. Your dedication won't change the snake into a panda bear.

If you are dating someone, and they show you their true colors or spew venom at you with their biting words, then you are seeing the real person. Don't try to love them into a better, emotionally healthy person. It won't work. It's nature vs. nurture, and in dating prospects, nature typically wins.

I believe people can change, but for the most part they don't. Why? It takes a lot of work and time to change. Psychologists have said that someone with a personality disorder, like narcissism, can only change their behaviors. And that takes years of solo counseling, group therapy, and couples therapy. And even then, most people do not change.

If Their Absence Brings You Peace, You Didn't Lose Them. They Lost You.

Did that person who exited your life leave you empty or relieved? There is a difference. Even if you feel sad yet at peace, then you didn't suffer a loss. They did. Give it a few days, and you'll feel better. Especially now that you continue to work on your "stuff" and your healing, you must protect your peace at all costs.

In our peace we access our strength and clarity about situations. We can make parenting and work decisions with more confidence. In our peace, we can access and hear our higher power.

Protect your peace. You're on the way to greatness.

Protect your energy

Your energy will be contagious now that you've done the healing process outlined in this book. Yes, you will still have a few bad days because life throws us curve balls. But for the most part, you are the best you have been after working through your past. People will be drawn to your energy and want to be around you more, including prospective love interests.

However, you must guard your energy with open eyes and care. Some people will be energy suckers and want to bring you down by taking in your good vibes. They may discount something you say or believe in. Then bam, you feel your energy shift. We can't let this happen.

If you know someone who calls you consistently to complain about how unfair life is, don't answer every time. This is your time to take care of you and keep the momentum going. You can absolutely return the call later but wait until you are strong and content before taking on yet another project.

There are many experts who talk about manifesting your best life by putting the right energy out into the universe. Abraham Hicks and Gabby Bernstein are two of my favorites. You can find them on YouTube, by the way. They believe that the more positive vibes you put out into the universe, the greater the probability that what you desire and deserve will come your way.

I believe this process. I have seen it happen in my own life. I am the happiest and most at peace I have ever been as I write this manuscript. I am spending less and less time with toxic people and other energy suckers. I am focusing on my relationship with my higher power, myself, my son, and my dreams. Guess what? I have more sales at work, more dates, more fun, and more peace because I choose who I let into my life.

Protect your energy because no one else will. You've done the healing work in the previous chapter, and hopefully you are feeling better and holding yourself accountable for what you've learned to do differently.

Stop Giving to People Who Don't Value You

Like many lessons in this book, this guidance can apply to anyone in your life, including friends, lovers, colleagues, and family. People will take and take from us and never reciprocate. Yet, we not only allow it to happen, but we also find ways to give and do more. We must stop that right now.

I believe there are two types of people on this earth: givers and takers. The takers will continue to steal our joy, peace, patience, and even money if we allow it to happen. We must put boundaries in place so this doesn't occur. This may mean that you lose that friend for good, or it may translate into family members being upset that you said, "No" for the first time in, well, forever. When you get pushback on your boundary, know that you have done something right. How are you going to date if you are empty?

I'll give you an example from my dating experiences. I was dating a guy off and on for two years. During the times we were together, I went to almost every Sprint car race his teenage son had, whether it was forty-five minutes or three hours away. I would leave work early and meet Matt at his apartment, and off we would go. We usually wouldn't get back to Dallas until 4 a.m.

If I add it up, I am guessing I attended at least twenty car races across Texas. How many of my son's basketball games did Matt attend? You guessed the correct answer: Zero. Who was the giver and who was the taker? I think I had a "G" for giver tattooed on my forehead during that relationship. There was absolutely no balance. Let people like this go.

They Don't See Your Value? Keep it Moving

You will date some people who just don't see all that you bring to the table. You may be beautiful outside and inside, intelligent, witty, kind, loving, appreciative, and more, but some people have blinders on. These men and women have usually been damaged in relationships in the past, or they have unrealistic standards. I know you want everyone to see your value and like you, but it's their vision problem, not yours.

Also, some people today want perfection because of what life appears to be on social media. The filters and special effects can make an average person look like a supermodel. Also, some people don't understand that social media offers a highlight reel of others' lives. That gorgeous holiday card where the family wore matching pajamas and drank hot cocoa? The parents had been fighting for an hour before the photographer snapped the picture. Yes, I know even the dog looked happy, but that's because Doggo had just eaten half a fruitcake and pooped on the carpet. You and I understand these things, but shallow people do not. They want magazine-worthy when that is never real. That's no loss for you. I know you think your love will change their minds, and you can show them how awesome you are. Don't put in the effort.

A great analogy is to not be a "pick me."

Keep it moving, gorgeous. There's authenticity and appreciation for you around the corner.

You Will Know When Someone Is Crazy about You

You won't be able to escape this person when they are into you. You will know they like you because they'll tell you. They'll ask you on dates. They'll call and text regularly. They'll want to know when your schedule is open so they can plan around it. Also, they'll offer to drive a long way to pick you up or meet you. They'll insist on paying for everything, from a nice dinner to cup of coffee. If you are on the giving end, the person you are chasing says yes to every opportunity to see you. Or, this person may respond with, "I can't Tuesday night, but I am free all day Wednesday." This person may also insist on reciprocating. This person wants to see you and invest their valuable time with you.

Here are signs to look for when you someone isn't into you. I know these hurt if you let them, but don't. It's better to know now they aren't the one for you. Keep it moving.

Inconsistencies – This person is inconsistent about communication. You may hear from them regularly for a week, then they fall off the face of the earth. They are so quiet you wonder if you should check the obituaries.

One of the reasons for this push and pull can be that this person is not ready to date. They see your value, get excited, and promise great dates with you, then they scare themselves silly. Or this person is not the commitment type. It just feels good to have you sliding into their DMs or text messages. Your face pops up, and they tell themselves they are worthy of you, even when they don't make a move. They are scared or toxic. Either way, next please.

This person was never really into you (or likely anyone else), no matter the excuse.

Disappears – The disappearing act used to get under my skin and stay there. A voice in my head would say, "See, Laura, you aren't worth it." But I changed that. I know now that these people, both men and women, are flakes. They will jump from person to person and meet more people online in a year than you and I could meet in a lifetime. It's about quantity, not quality for them. Remind yourself this is good. Because you are too valuable for their apathy and indecisiveness. You don't get second and third chances with people like you.

Second chances - I have given two men I loved second chances to come back and try the relationship again. Both times the guys said the right things, and I agreed to give it another shot. The first time, it was Doug who pursued me a second time. He said he could tell that I was a different person after letting time pass since my divorce. And the second guy came in hot, telling me he was ready for me now and that he had grown a lot. Here's what happened in both situations: It didn't work. Both times were a disaster, ending once again in broken heart.

Dr. Dharius Daniels said this: "Don't go back if the reason you left is still there."

Ask yourself these questions before giving someone a second chance:

- Have they changed? Have they done the challenging work to work on themselves? Have they gone to counseling or support groups?

- What is different this time that will make it work? What are the actions of this person that are different? Remember, actions over words in the dating world.

- Can I give this person a second chance without a detrimental breakup if things go sideways again?

- How much did this person hurt me last time?

- Did I forget and deify this person? Go back and write down all the negative traits. Ask yourself what's still there and what's not.

Do these things and then make your decision. My mom had a choice to make when she was in college that decided her future, although she didn't know it at the time. My dad was downstairs in her dorm, waiting to see her, but the guy who had broken her heart was on the phone. My dad's actions had shown he was solid and committed. This guy, Bill, had hurt her over and over. She chose my dad that day. They've been married fifty-two years.

Ladies, Don't Consider It Monogamous Until HE Locks You Down

There are so many times that women have come to me in tears, hurting because they have been sleeping with a guy, traveling with a guy, or spending most of their free time with a guy, only to find out he is still seeing other women. Ladies, just because you went to Mexico with him, it doesn't mean he isn't communicating with others. Also, just because you have mind-blowing sex with him, it doesn't mean he isn't doing that with someone else.

When does it mean he is devoted solely to you? Well, when he says he wants to date you and only you. He asks for monogamy. The thought of you being with another man drives him crazy, and he wants you all to himself.

If this isn't the case, you can't take it personally. Some men are not ready to settle down or may never be. One guy may not be in love with you no matter how amazing you are. Again, you're not going to be for everybody, and everyone isn't going to be for you. Think of the hearts you've broken, ladies.

If you are like me and you get attached or catch feelings after sleeping with someone, then don't until you know there's a commitment. This is another way of protecting your heart.

If you can go on a fabulous trip and have great sex without getting attached, then pack your bags and be realistic. Enjoy the moment with no judgment here. I wish I had a thicker skin! Remember, though, that he might be taking another trip with someone else next weekend.

The Dating Cycle

Let's say you've met someone who appears to be an incredible person, because you will meet that person. Ask enough questions to find out where they are in the dating cycle.

The dating cycle is a theory my good friend Michael, an attorney, developed after he had been in the dating world off and on for a decade. Michael told me he always asks clarifying questions to learn how long a date has been divorced, separated, or single. Many people who have recently exited a long relationship often go a little crazy at first, dating as much and as often as they can. Many men and women feel like they've been thrown into a candy store full of people ready to date, laugh, have fun, and enjoy sex. It's an overwhelming sense of freedom, especially after a long marriage or relationship. Only when and if the shine wears off, is when people see that the dating world isn't only about quantity. It's about quality. That quality for someone may be a pretty face, youth, spiritual connectedness, wealth, or intelligence, but people either decide they want to pursue that something more or keep playing the game. It's up to us to decide what we want to do.

If a person is recently separated or divorced, Michael and I share this piece of advice: Don't date them. They are likely a hot mess. Separation or divorce is ranked as the second most painful life event right after the death of a spouse.[22]

Give this person some time to heal. They may say, "Oh I healed a long time ago." Um . . . no. Give them a year or so. You can have fun with them or hang out with them but be careful about getting into a relationship with someone who has recently gone through that trauma. Remember, hurt people hurt people. Protect yourself.

WHEN YOU GET SERIOUS WITH SOMEONE

1. Ask them to go to therapy, like you do.

At this point in the book, you know how much I believe in therapy and coaching. Even if all you can afford is a session once a month, it's important to have someone who can help you understand your feelings and struggles. Therapists will typically call you out when you are lying to yourself or others. A good therapist will cheer for you, while making sure you are being honest with others and yourself.

If your person doesn't want to go to therapy, I would think long and hard before moving in with or marrying them. If someone doesn't have the ability to look at their own issues or wrong doings, then they have no self-awareness. This means, in the future, they may make everything your fault. They will take no responsibility for financial issues, family matters, sick kids, infidelity, or any major issue that arises. A healthy relationship comprises two people who take responsibility for what is their "stuff." They follow that up with a healthy apology.

2. Meet their family and friends.

You can learn a lot by meeting the family of the one you love. There are genetic tendencies in families and patterns that you can witness by simply sharing a meal or two with them. You may see a dynamic between men and women that you otherwise wouldn't see.

It could be that the woman prepares the meal each time and the men clean up the kitchen, or vice versa. My sweet paternal grandmother never cooked, but she was the one who nurtured the children, bandaged up wounds, helped with homework, and drove the kids to piano and school. My grandfather enjoyed cooking, especially in his later years.

Also, you may witness dynamics that you don't find attractive or healthy. In my Texas suburb last week, I saw a husband and wife walking down the sidewalk. The woman was six feet behind the man. This could be a cultural appropriation or an expectation. You need to determine if such beliefs work for you.

Finally, there is a proverb that says, "A man is judged by the company he keeps." Look at your prospective partner's friends. Do they act with integrity? Character? Do they have a work ethic that you agree with? How do they treat people of the opposite sex? Or nonbinary people? Are they judgmental? Do they party too much? These are insights into someone's character and way of life. Decide if it's right for you.

3. Date your potential partner for a minimum of two years or eight seasons.

I think this is some of the best advice that a counselor gave me. Unfortunately, it came after my divorce. I doubt I would've listened anyway because I wanted to be in love. I walked down the aisle thinking my marriage had a 50 percent chance of working. And I am not kidding. I wish I had followed this advice from the beginning.

It is difficult for a toxic person to keep a mask on for more than two years. That's two holiday seasons, two spring breaks, two winters, and two summers. Of course, this list goes on. That's 730 days to watch someone navigate life. You can learn a lot about a person over two years, yet you still won't know everything. Some clients of mine were married thirty years before realizing whom they were really married to. Can you imagine marrying someone in a few short months, then you realize years later they have two families? Or perhaps you learn they have grown children with a baby daddy you never knew about? Finally, maybe you discover they work for the CIA in counterintelligence, and an adversary knows where you live? I know these are extreme examples, but I think they drive home my point. Patience reaps rewards in your future. Use time as a gift and not a hindrance.

4. Watch for codependency.

This is an all-too common dynamic that takes place in relationships. For this book, I interviewed several psychologists who chose not to be identified, and this came up several times.

Codependency is when a relationship is off-balance. One person has significantly more power in the relationship than the other and often takes advantage of that consciously or unconsciously. The giving person in the relationship often loses sight of how much they're giving and trying to rescue someone. The giver ends up emotionally depleted and loses their sense of self. The taker's needs, wants, and desires become the sole focus of the relationship, with the giver becoming a victim by a blind, generous choice.

5. Be authentic to yourself.

We all put our best foot forward when we meet someone. One of my best friends says we have on "our church clothes." But here's the trick to a healthy relationship: Be who you are from the beginning. You can be your best self, but be authentic to you. Don't become a chameleon.

You can be your best self, but be authentic to you.

It's easy when you fall for someone to be the first to volunteer to change things about yourself. Maybe you are terrified of sky diving because you have a fear of heights, but you do it to please your partner. Or maybe you are a Christiaan, but you've fallen for someone who is Jewish. So, without being asked, you convert to Judaism. The trouble comes when we make life-changing decisions, and the relationship doesn't last. Not only are we left disappointed and hurt, but we also have more reckless choices to reverse.

There is someone out there who will adore that you are afraid of heights or someone that cherishes that you were brought up in Sunday school. Don't settle, and don't change.

CHAPTER 13

TALKING ABOUT SEX AND AVOIDING NUDES

Y ou know we need to talk about this, and I was surprised as I was writing this book that this topic needs its own chapter. Welcome to the new truth about dating!

I learned once that couples argue over money, sex, religion, kids, and politics more than any other topics. Do not be embarrassed as we get down to the nitty gritty. This is important stuff.

Sex

There are people who date for sex only. And when I mean only, as soon as they sleep with you, they're gone. Literally and figuratively, they disappear. They leave your home and your inbox all in the same few hours, and you never see them again. Many of these people find other people who just want to have sex. If that works for you, great. Please use protection and expect nothing emotionally. To me that's the short game, and I am more interested in the long game. I want to slowly move toward the goal line of a relationship.

> You'll need love, compassion, interest, and commitment. That's the glue that keeps the relationship in one piece.

When do you sleep with someone you like? That is entirely up to you, but the longer you wait, the more stable your relationship can be. I know you feel closer to this person after being intimate with them, but you are risking the time it takes to develop the emotional glue that holds the relationship together. The great sex may always be there, but sometimes, it won't be enough to salvage a withering relationship. You will need more. You'll need love, compassion, interest, and commitment. That's the glue that keeps the relationship in one piece.

Science reinforces that closeness. Studies have shown that oxytocin, released during sex, not only makes you feel closer to your mate, but it also prevents you from becoming close to other potential mates, helping to maintain fidelity.

Men and the Emotional Connection

Recent studies show that visual images arouse men when it comes to sex, such as seeing a partner in a sexy lingerie. For some men, porn works. However, these same studies show that men are less stimulated over time with the same images. Sometimes, men can desire sex for comfort, connection, or an ego boost, especially when they believe their partner is more attractive than they are. The bottom line is this: men don't think about an emotional connection first.

Most women, however, need to feel emotionally connected to have sex. Sure, there are those times when we just want sex and a warm body next to us, but for every encounter, we get a little attached. The serotonin and dopamine rushes are addictive, and we feel like we've left a little of ourselves behind with each person we've slept with.

To me, it's the worst to know that I slept with someone who doesn't want a commitment. It's difficult to imagine him seeing me on a Friday and "her" on a Saturday. Unless there's a discussion about the relationship and monogamy, I don't go there. My heart won't take it. I have friends who are tougher and enjoy sex just to have sex. And good for them. I am wired differently, which serves me well sometimes and not so well others.

I learned this, too, from my former coach. Men think clearly after sex, but women think clearly before. Once women have sex, it muddies the relationship for us. We get closer, want more of an emotional connection, and become attached.

Men think clearly after sex, but women think clearly before.

Nudes - Dick Pics and More

A survey done in 2019 by researchers at Bumble,[23] the dating app, revealed that one in three women have received a dick pic while dating online. These women received pictures of a man's penis from all angles via air drop from a stranger on a subway or in-app messaging. Ninety six percent said the dick pics were received without their consent. Listen, guys. If you've sent a dick pic to your girlfriend, and she responded with a nude, then that's not what I am talking about here. This is when this flagrant act pops up in a woman's messages, and the woman didn't ask for it.

I have been one of those women to receive dick pics after one or two text messages. "Do you want this?" some men will say. Others will ask, "What are you doing?" I answer, "Not you."

Anyway, as the recipient of this brazen art, I either delete the pics or forward them to my bestie and go "another one." (Don't judge. I am not the only woman who does this. Sometimes we just don't want to feel alone in receiving what is the equivalent of being flashed on a public street.)

Guys, you may need to think more here unless you aren't embarrassed. You may hope that your penis pic makes it to the eyes of a woman you're pursuing, but it also may make it to forty-seven of her closest friends. And sometimes the woman who would've slept with you runs in the other direction.

Some states have legislation in place that makes it illegal to send an unsolicited pic of a body part. "Cyber flashing" in Texas can lead to a Class C Misdemeanor and a $500 fine. This legislation was spearheaded by Bumble CEO and Founder Whitney Wolfe, who grew up and lives in Texas.

On a side note, research published in the Journal of Sex Research in July 2019 found that those who send nudes are likely to be narcissists. One thousand and eighty-seven men completed an online survey that asked about their sexual proclivities and reasons for any exhibitionism. After reviewing the finds, researchers wrote, "*We determined that the most frequently reported motivational category for sending genital images was a transactional mindset (i.e., motivated by hopes of receiving images in return), while the most desired reaction from recipients was that of sexual excitement. Further, we determined that men who reported having sent unsolicited dick pics demonstrated higher levels of narcissism and endorsed greater ambivalent and hostile sexism than their non-sending counterparts.*"[24]

What do you do? Again, think of your friend. The window is short for people who just want sex. After two or three dates without sex, you can almost be guaranteed that person will move on if it's only intercourse that they're after. If you're not sure, go on at least three dates with a person before thinking about having sex with them. If they stick around till the fourth or fifth date, they are more likely to want more than just sex with you. Don't take this personally either. When someone wants sex, they are focused on it and will move on quickly to get it. They weren't for you. Let them keep their tally going. You keep your chin up as you find the love of your life. We all get old, and our parts don't work like we want them to. You'll be in a committed relationship, while the other person is still floundering in the dating pond, going from meaningless hookup to hookup.

More Than You Bargain For

This is a touchy subject, so I am going to write about it in short and concise language. If you are dating someone, and they begin to talk about kinky sex, threesomes, and other sexual escapades early on, then they may be into some sexual partnerships you aren't interested in or want. They are giving you the tip of the iceberg.

Anecdotally, I have seen this. I dated a guy whose friend, James, often hired women thirty years younger to accompany him on outings, dates, and for sexual experiences. This guy also went to sex and swinger parties where couples traded off and engaged in orgies. I never asked where nor did I want to know. I am warning you because seeing someone so open and unashamed about their sex lives early on may indicate what they are doing is far more than you want. You may be thinking that a person like this won't like the typical dating app. Think again. I saw this particular dude on an app last year when I was single. Keep it moving, ladies and gentlemen. If that's a red flag in the beginning, it's not going to turn white, no matter how much you bleach it.

CHAPTER 14

RECOGNIZING YOUR ENDGAME

Proverbs 4:23: Above all else, guard your heart,
because everything you do flows from it.

Several years ago, my friend Heather wanted to get remarried more than anything else in life. She was obsessed with finding her next husband. Heather's first marriage had ended in divorce due to infidelity by her spouse, but she still believed in true love, so much so that she shopped for engagement rings during her lunch hour at work. She was frustrated, though, because she hadn't found her groom. By the way, I love her commitment to finding true, unconditional love, because I also believe it exists. However, we can't make it happen or force it. Heather was doing both.

A few months after her jewelry shopping experience, Heather began dating a guy she met on Bumble. Javier seemed to check every box, at least at first. As the relationship progressed, she found it more difficult to feel the chemistry with Javier because his actions were turning her off. For example, Javier seldom had his twelve-year-old son over to spend the night, despite what the divorce agreement dictated. Heather's life focused on first, finding a husband, and second, her children. She couldn't understand how and why Javier didn't want to see or fight to see his son.

Also, Javier liked to mention his home country of Venezuela in every conversation, insinuating that his country was superior to the United States. Javier also talked about money a lot, which drove Heather crazy.

One day, Heather called and said, "We've been getting serious, you know? And Javier is driving me crazy with almost everything he does. Even the way he chews his food bothers me."

I asked Heather if she felt like she was trying to force something. She admitted yes, she was. I shared with Heather some of my father's best wisdom: you can't fit a square peg in a round hole. If it's not working, it's not working. Heather should have been crazy about Javier at this point because it was still early in the relationship. Yet, Heather wanted to find a husband so badly, she was willing to sacrifice many things that were important to her. She was going to settle.

In the end she didn't settle. She told Javier why she was ending their relationship. I was happy for her because she is a gorgeous, smart, and giving person. She deserved more.

No one is perfect, and I am not insinuating that you can find a perfect person. There's no perfect couple, either. However, you can find a partner perfect for you.

Settling

Settling means accepting things in a relationship that you deeply know are wrong for you.

THERE ARE SEVERAL REASONS PEOPLE SETTLE.

1. They don't want to be alone.

I get it. It's scary doing everything by yourself without a backup. There's also the fear of diving back in the dating pool. *However, don't let your emotions dictate your future.* Fear will fade with each step you take as a single person. Also, what if you are missing "your person" because you are settling for someone else? You will never know if you stay with "okay."

2. They are attached to a time or relationship for sentimental reasons.

Maybe the relationship reminds you of a difficult relationship you had with a parent. In your own way, you are trying to heal from that while acting out the same scenario in your adulthood. *Forgive your past and focus on the future.* Drop the baggage so you don't end up in a relationship that is worse than the one you experienced when you were young.

3. They say the person is "good enough."

What if you buy a gallon of oat milk at the store mistaking it for vanilla milk? You get in the car, open it, and take a big slug. For some reason it's not vanilla; in fact, it has no flavor at all. And you know the store manager may not agree to reimburse you because it's open. So, you accept your plight and drive home thinking, my cereal will suck tomorrow morning, but at least it's healthy enough to drink. Get it? Why have plain when you can have a strong, French vanilla milk?

Signs You Are Settling:

1. You pick apart your mate.

Nothing your partner does makes you happy. Even the trivial things irritate you. You begin to get angry with your partner more often, straining the relationship. I find that usually the person who feels they aren't settling is the one more invested in the relationship. Yes, you may break a heart if you leave this person now, but it's better than a trip later to a divorce attorney.

2. You make excuses for this person.

Also, if you find yourself making excuses for this person, do a self-check. Is what you are seeing part of a pattern? Maybe you tell yourself often that, "It's okay that they're always late," or "they really didn't mean the ugly remark they just said." This may happen occasionally, but if this is a pattern, at our ages it's not going to change. Even with a lot of work and therapy, it is challenging to change a person who has established patterns they have been comfortable with for years or decades.

3. You ask others if this person is the one.

You shouldn't have to ask. If you are ready for a relationship, and you've met the person for you, you will know. In fact, if a friend begins to criticize your new partner, you will likely get pissed off and walk away. After you've done your homework on this person through a background check, your dating checklist, and other people who know them well, you just know. You remove the dating apps and cannot wait to continue to build on what you have.

4. You ask yourself if you are settling.

You may be asking yourself, "How in the world do I tell the difference?" This is where you listen to your instincts and intuition. If your brain is telling you this is a good person, but your body and instincts are saying I feel no chemistry with this person and their habits bug me, then exit stage left.

People often tell me, "But Laura, I feel like I need to settle so I can get married!" I get it. I had doubts but married anyway, and look how it worked out for me. (It wasn't good, let's just say. My book *Ugly Love* recaps those painfully difficult sixteen years.)

Don't settle.

Where is God in Dating?

I have been fortunate to work with Rebecca Lynn Pope and recently, Dr. Dharius Daniels. Daniels is a transformational coach, author, and pastor. Dr. Daniels changed my life in the last year, as well as the lives of my colleagues in his mastermind group, through his honest teachings and encouragement.

The quote that sticks out the most is about our generational strongholds: "If it still has hold of you, it likely didn't come from you." These are the strongholds that can hurt our dating potential if we don't address them through therapy or coaching.

A second quote from Dr. Daniels that resonates with me today is, "Fear makes you prophesize the wrong outcome." I often get in my head and overthink my future, instead of enjoying today and celebrating what has happened so far. Where your mind goes is where you go!

Finally, I know that we can get hurt anywhere. I am not telling you to date someone religious because the person I met in church hurt me worse than I've ever been hurt. It's important to make sure you are yoked the same way financially, religiously, physically, and mentally.

This shows us that we can be hurt no matter where we meet people. We must guard our hearts! Again, Proverbs 4:23: *Above all else, guard you heart, because everything you do flows from it.*

That verse says it all. In the secular space, Dr. Phil wrote in his book *Life Code*[25] that we must meet someone and not immediately decide whether this person is good or bad. We are neutral. We don't judge, but we wait and let themselves prove what they are. Slow down. The slower you go in learning things about someone before being intimate with them, the more you will learn. Again, slow is fast and fast is slow.

God will be in your dating life as much as you want Him to be. And sometimes, He will intervene even when you don't want His assistance. I believe if God isn't in the relationship, it won't work.

If you are unsure about a person or event or even a first date, pray. Ask God to show you what you need to do. And like with Jeffrey and the cans of Red Bull, He will. It may not be the answer you want, but I promise, later, you'll be relieved that relationship didn't work out. As Dr. Daniels says, "God sits high and looks low." God can see the future, including your perfect mate. That's why things happen that we don't understand. He may let us endure a little pain now instead of an enormous amount of heartache later. Can you imagine if I had married Doug from earlier in this book? We would certainly be divorced by now, or I would be miserable.

Also, when you face rejection, before you turn to your amazing friends, turn to God. He wants to comfort you and reveal your next steps. Some of the verbiage I repeat to myself after rejection, and again attributed to Dr. Dharius, are:

God redeems time.

That last statement has rescued me many times over the years. I can be in a sinking ship in a sea of emotions, and that phrase comes to me: God redeems time.

Personal examples of this abound for me. Anytime I feel like I am behind—perhaps a relationship didn't work out, or I didn't get the job I thought I wanted—God shows me later that those things weren't meant to happen. He consistently blows my mind with things that follow a huge disappointment, especially in my personal life. Guess why *Ugly Love* was written? I was healing from the breakup with Doug. I took a time-out from dating and decided to listen to God's nudge that I needed to write about my abusive past. A few hours that book was released, it became a number one best seller.

If I hadn't gone through the destruction of that relationship, I wouldn't have drawn closer to God and published a book. I was so focused on my man, who I can see now was quite demanding, that I never would have written the manuscript and started a YouTube channel that grew to half a million subscribers. It doesn't mean that my breakup was an easy recovery. In fact, it was the opposite. I cried every day and lost ten pounds. But, looking back, I dodged a bullet and found my calling.

On that note, guess why I sat down to write this manuscript? It wasn't because I was bored. It's because I dated a guy off and on for two years that hurt me because I was vulnerable too soon. *I fell in love with who he pretended to be.* He talked about marriage. He got to know my son. My son liked this guy. We both got hurt.

That's why I decided to share what I've learned from dating, the good and the bad, so you don't make the same mistakes. It took me almost a year to get better. You don't deserve that.

God can do things in your life that aren't possible without Him. Don't feel like you've wasted a minute getting to this point. You are right where you need to be! When I feel down about something, I go to Romans 8:28 in the Bible: *And we know that in all things God works for the good of those who love him, who have been called according to his purpose.*

What Do I Do in the Meantime?

Bottom line: Live your best life now. Don't wait on a man or woman to come into the picture. Travel. Work hard or don't work. Make friends. Date around. Live big and not small. It's when you are living your best life that you attract the best for you. And until that person knocks you off your feet, don't stop living a life of your dreams, built and orchestrated by you.

Here is my mantra, and you might want to live by this, too.

There are only a lucky few who are invited into my life and into my inner circle. My time is my most valuable asset. Only people who have proven themselves or can be a in a mutually beneficial relationship have access to me. If I must question someone's character or intentions, they aren't allowed in my circle. Period. If you don't get my back, then you don't get the benefits of me. I will ask you to leave, and there's no negotiation. I am tired of recovering from narcissists and other toxic people. Life is short. Joy, peace, and love are my priorities. Nothing will take that away. Nothing.

The Endgame

The endgame is when you know without a doubt you've found your person. You love and care for each other deeply, and you cannot imagine your life without them. That's your endgame. My good friend and former coach

Rebecca put it this way: "I cannot imagine my life without my husband, Kerry. He means so much to me. If something happened to him, I wouldn't get married again. I don't think I would get over it and remarry."

The answer to finding the love of your life is not to settle for something that's not perfect for you. Again, we're not talking about a perfect person. That person doesn't exist. Settling in a relationship is not the place God has for you. You will have zero doubt when you meet that person.

There is someone out there who will love you right, and you will love them in return. There's someone who will love your faults, applaud your strengths, hold you when you cry, and celebrate your victories. This person will think you are the best thing to ever walk this earth. And this person will thank God for bringing you to them. They are your best friend, your love, your soulmate, and your forever.

DATING STORY #8

"Catfished by Calamari Man"

I had to end with one more!

Three years ago, I met a guy on Bumble named Greg. His profile pictures showed he was tall, blond, handsome, and had a great smile. Greg listed his age as forty-nine and his hometown as Dallas. We texted through the app for a few days, and on a Tuesday, Greg asked me out for a drink on Friday. I said yes.

When I arrived at the appointed Mexican food restaurant near the Four Seasons Hotel around 5 p.m., I headed for the bar, where Greg had asked to meet. I did a loop around the area, and I didn't see my date. There were a few couples, an older gentleman with grey hair wearing a tweed sportscoat, and the bartender. I thought to myself, "Surely I haven't been stood up." I did another lap, and while I was looking at the patrons, the grey-haired man stood up.

"Laura, I am right here," Greg said.

Immediately I knew that Greg had posted pictures from ten years and forty (less) pounds ago. I chastised myself for being judgmental, then encouraged myself to enjoy his company. He could be a nice man, I thought.

We ordered margaritas, and Greg insisted I try the calamari. I said thanks, but I am not hungry. He ordered it anyway.

I love calamari, but a few minutes later our appetizer arrived, and the squid was almost swimming on the plate in a thick ocean of grease. It didn't look like something I would enjoy, so again, I politely declined. Greg decided forcing me to try the squid was the best route, so he took a forkful and shoved it toward my mouth.

"Bartender," Greg said. "Tell Laura she will love the calamari. And please give us more secret sauce."

The bartender looked at me with these big, watery, soulful eyes, and he shrugged a little. I could tell the guy felt sorry for me. There wasn't enough secret sauce in the world to make me enjoy this date.

I chewed the calamari he shoved in my mouth for what seemed like an hour, and finally, I choked it down. At this point, I was pissed. No one makes me eat, drink, or do something I don't want to do. Last I checked, I was an adult who makes her own choices on just about all aspects of her life.

I finished the rest of the margarita in about five seconds and told Greg I needed to leave. Ever the gentleman (sarcasm here), Greg walked me to my car, and he said he would reach out later because he wanted to see me again. I politely said, "I had a great time, but I don't think we're a match." I drove off, and a couple of minutes later, my phone was blowing up with text messages.

"How dare you say we're not a match," Greg wrote. "You don't know what you're missing."

Not surprisingly, I did know what I would be missing: Oily calamari and an angry, aggressive man with no self-awareness.

At this point, I was getting plucky. I wrote back, "Greg, first your pictures were from 1987. That's not cool. You misrepresented yourself so therefore catfished me. That's strike one. Secondly, don't ever make a woman do something when she says 'no.' You're lucky I didn't choke and die on the squid."

Then I blocked him.

The next day, during a sales call, my phone started blowing up from an unknown number. It was Greg. He had texted me from another phone so he could accuse me of being high maintenance, rude, and needy. I didn't respond to this tirade, but simply blocked him on this number, too.

Do I eat calamari now? I think you know the answer to that.

THANK YOU

The dating world is no joke, as I've explained in this book. I didn't think I had another book in me, but God kept giving me a nudge and saying, "Look how far you've come and look how strong you are. You need to share this with others." Reluctantly, I sat down to write eight months ago. Two eye surgeries later, not because of writing but just life, I finished the manuscript. You can thank the Lord for what this book teaches you. In addition to the huge thank you to the Lord, I need to thank Dr. Dharius Daniels and his wife, Pastor Shameka. I attended several leadership meetings and joined a few of his leadership groups in which Pastor Shameka and "Pastor Dharius both taught. This couple is a powerhouse that leads a church of predominantly single members. I found Dr. Dharius when I was going through my divorce, and anytime I need to hear from God, I pull up one of his sermons and the answer is right in front of me. Also, I need to thank Laquonne Holden for his leadership in our i3 group. Pastor Laquonne is a superstar, a gift, and a blessing to so many around him. Finally, I need to thank all the people I met in i3, especially Doctors Fatimah and Vernell. These women are the epitome of strong, kind, Christian women. They are also some of the funniest people I've met on this earth. I love you girls. I also need to thank the three people that have supported me, including one for thirty years. Thank you to Doctors Ray Levy and Shawn Lee for your insight and guidance though the last several years. Rebecca Lynn Pope, as I've told you a gazillion times, and yes that's a word, you've changed my life in so many ways. A thank you to my parents who look at me like I'm crazy sometimes but support me nonetheless. You are loving parents and a wonderful SuSu and Pawpaw. To my immediate posse in the suburbs where I live, you are so appreciated. Wyatt, Elizabeth, Holly, Kim, and Gigi, I thank you for your unconditional love, support, and humor. Also, to my friend Amy, I can't wait to hear you laugh out loud at some of the dating stories I haven't yet told you. My smart, kind, empathetic, athletic, and hilarious son—You are my reason for living. You are my greatest gift from God. From your early morning grumpiness to your nicknames for me, you keep me on my toes. You call me "Gorch," so know that Gorch will always love you. I am your ride or die. Finally, thank you to *you*, the single person who bought this book. Don't let any man or woman define your worth. You are special just like you are. Keep going and everything will fall into place. Your person is out there waiting for their person, which is you.

REFERENCES

1. https://www.news.standford.edu

2. https://www.businessofapps.com/dating

3. https://www.gillespieshields.com

4. https://www.businessofapps.com/dating

5. https://www.onlinelibrary.wiley.com/doi/full/10.1111/ sjop.12631

6. https://www.americanaddictioncenters.org

7. https://www.Helenfisher.com

8. https://www.brainyquotes.com

9. https://www/.psychologytoday.com

10. https://www.psychealive.org

11. https://www.psychologytoday.com

12. https://stylecaster.com/dating-trends-2022/

13. https://www.uscornhole.com

14. *Single and Secure*, Rich Wilkerson Jr, VOUS Church Publishing, January 1, 2022.

15. https://www.link.springer.com

16. https://www.singlesreports.com

17. https://www.gottman.com

18. *Diagnostic and Statistical Manual of Mental Health Disorders*, Fifth Edition. American Psychiatric Association. Rock City Books. December 1, 2022.

19. https://www.scienceofpeople.com/red-flags/

20. https://stylecaster.com/dating-trends-2022/

21. *The Power of the Pussy*. Aitken House Publishing. July 24, 2014.

22. https://www.stress.org

23. https://www.insider.com

24. https://www.researchgate.net

25. *Life Code*, Dr. Phil McGraw, Bird Street Books. February 12, 2013.